Fiftee [illegible] of Retirement Success

Second Edition

Richard P. Johnson, Ph.D.
Warren E. Jensen, D.Min.

KENDALL/HUNT PUBLISHING COMPANY
4050 Westmark Drive Dubuque, Iowa 52002

ISBN 0-7872-2884-2

Printed in the United States of America
10 9 8 7 6 5 4 3 2

❖ Acknowledgments ❖

We believe this book will make a significant contribution to the retirement well-being of many people. It could not have been completed without the help and cooperation of many people, Chief among these in my life are:

Kathie Dawley – my wife, colleague and source of encouragement throughout this writing,

John Dawley – one of my family who supplied never ending technical assistance in the computer analysis of statistical data,

Carla Jensen – another family member who patiently and professionally helped our text to become readable,

To all my early friends and clients at Meredith Corporation for helping us establish the statistical foundation so essential to this program.

Warren E. Jensen, D. Min.

To Sandra – my wife and support-mate throughout the writing and conversations about this book. Without her endless hours of computer programming, enabling a complicated idea to become practical and available to so many people, this book would not have been possible. Without her, it could not have been completed!

Richard P. Johnson, Ph.D.

❖ Contents ❖

❖ Preface ❖

Retirement Planning . . . More than Money!

We believe that forming a plan for a successful retirement is much like constructing a beautiful building. A building first needs a strong foundation to keep it standing straight. It requires a sturdy support structure of beams, joists and trusses to keep it from toppling over. Further, it requires a leakproof roof to keep it dry, and functional siding and insulation to keep the weather outside. It needs windows for light and doors for access. It requires painting for protection, walkways for easier access, and landscaping for enhanced beauty. Inside it needs furniture, fixtures, elevators, stairs, hallways, room dividers and floors. A building requires many different materials and a lot of "know how" to build it into a thing of long lasting function and pleasing beauty . . . a place where people can be happy.

To construct a successful retirement life you also need many different materials, just like with your building. The foundation of your retirement plan is your financial situation. Sometimes it's tempting to believe that retirement preparation is simply a matter of good financial planning alone. Nothing could be further from the truth. Beyond finances are the fourteen other retirement success factors which form the superstructure, the roof, windows, and everything you'll need to make your retirement as successful as your life has been so far. With this book you will identify and measure all 15 retirement success factors (including "perception of financial preparation") which are the building materials for your successful retirement. You will gain a solid understanding of the materials you already have, so that you, as the master builder of your own retirement, will know what more you might need as well as how to make these materials the best possible quality. You will have all the "know-how" you need to build your retirement phase of life into something both functional and beautiful.

A few weeks ago we were invited to attend an "Over the Hill" surprise birthday party. It was being held to commemorate the 50th birthday of a good friend. The instructions for the party were simple. Don't say anything to him before the party that might give away the surprise! Don't park in front of the house! Don't eat dinner before the party! And, bring a gag gift suitable for someone's 50th birthday celebration! We thought we could handle that! We even volunteered to do some shopping. What a cultural lesson we were about to receive!

Have you ever been invited to one of these parties? They are often held to recognize one's aging process as they move from one decade to another. Some folks are lucky enough to be honored this way as early as age thirty. Most, however, must wait to have this experience until they are forty or fifty. We've now gone to a number of these "celebrations" and have made what I think are some rather interesting observations about how we deal with aging in this culture.

When people mark the decade of their thirties, they often do so with a mood of challenge and enthusiasm. They have laid the groundwork for their careers and developed some long range goals. It's time to get busy and meet those goals! When people move into their forties, there seems to be a bit of anxiety or even fear about the future. You begin to hear jokes about getting old and a few black balloons begin to show up. There is a touch of realism and sobriety in the air! But, when one reaches the age of fifty!—WHOO-EEE!—it's all over. The mood is somber, sober, and quiet. People work at having fun and the gifts reflect the mood. Black balloons with hostile slogans printed on them—canes and crutches to remind the helpless victim of the "Grim Reaper" and the slow but steady aging process that just keeps coming. "Over the Hill" slogans and signs seem to be everywhere! Black crepe paper, sympathy cards, and some rather hostile sexual cards reflecting life experiences that now supposedly will be only memories of a distant past. Often there is too much liquor used for forgetting problems and too little dancing to celebrate life. I strongly suspect these cultural "rites of passage" reflect strong feelings and ideas about life and death that influence everyone's experiences of life. And not in a positive way!

Aging happens to all of us. No one escapes it because it is part of our life cycle. We are given this gift of life to use and enjoy. As we mature, we look for increasing meaning and deeper reasons for this gift. Because many others have made this pilgrimage before us, there are clues along the path. We pick them up and use them to form our own belief system that better explains the meaning of this gift of life. Sometimes the clues are helpful to us; sometimes they inhibit our attempts to find deeper meanings.

We hope you have chosen to read this book because you are still looking for clues! Or, better yet, we hope you've selected this book because you're ready to look at life through a different window. Sometimes the perspective you form from one direction does not help. When that happens you need to get a radically different point of view. If you can not change the window you've been looking through, put a different frame around the old one! We believe it's good to do that once in a while. For many people, it's long overdue.

Many of us carry beliefs and ideas around in our heads about the meaning of life and death that we inherited from our ancestors. Some of these need to be changed and updated because they restrict and limit our perspective on life and our potential to live it to its fullest. What we believe about getting older or aging certainly affects they way we plan for and approach retirement. Our belief system is crucial to the success of any plan we might draw up for our lives.

Do you remember that old story about the lady who always cut off the end of the rump roast before she put it in the pan? One day one of her granddaughters found herself cutting off the end of the rump roast she was cooking and paused to ask herself why she was doing that. Not having an answer, she called her mother and asked her why she had been taught to cook a rump roast that way. Somehow it did not make sense to be doing that! Her mother, in turn, said she did not really know, but that was the way her mother had done it. Undeterred, the young woman called her grandmother and asked her. Her grandmother, in turn said, "Why, I guess I learned it from my mother. One day I asked her why she did it and she said it was because her pan was too small to cook the roast in unless she cut the end off. I guess I've been doing it ever since without really thinking about it!"

This story is told only to remind you that sometimes you do things without thinking about the reasons, and sometimes you believe things without verifying the issues that formulated those beliefs. An example of this can be found in the belief system that you have developed around aging and retirement. We believe it is reflected in our "over the hill" parties. A few generations ago, our ancestors worked until they died. They really didn't think about retiring. They may have slowed down a bit, or did fewer things, but they did not really retire. When one retired, he/she usually did not live long. When you stopped working, it was because you could not go on any longer and you died. That was the way life was! And this is our history! And it is not to be thought of as ancient history. In 1925 the average life span was about 50 years. Now it's around 77 and rising!

The Center for Retirement Success, Inc., is convinced that our mind set is still reflecting the beliefs about retiring and aging, that were planted in our minds years ago. Retiring meant you were getting old, and when you got old, life was over in terms of enjoyment and purpose. And when life was over, you died! That scenario rings a familiar bell in the minds of many people. For most of us it does. That is the reason it is timely for you now to take another look at your beliefs about aging and retirement and evaluate them in the light of information relevant to today! Our world, obviously, is not the same world our grandparents and ancestors lived in and who then passed to us their beliefs and ideas. Our beliefs need to be based on the reality of our own world experience. If they are not, then we are looking out the wrong window!

So, What is the Reality of Today's World?

1. Recent U.S. Census Bureau statistics point to the fact that since the beginning of this century, life expectancy has increased almost 30 years! Projec-

tions show that women, by the year 2020 will have a life expectancy of almost 80 years, while men will lag about 6 1/2 years behind.

2. Currently, about 12.8% of the U.S. population of 257 million people is 65 or older. By the year 2020, this figure is projected to increase 17%, or to a total of 54 million people 65+, of the anticipated U.S. population figure of 324 million!
3. The fastest growth spot among the 65+ population is found among the very old. In 1990, 3 million people were 85 or older, representing about 1.2% of the total population figure. This is twice the proportion of this age category counted in 1960 and 6 times larger than that recorded in 1900!
4. In the next half-century, the number of Americans older than 85 may grow to nearly 24 million—twice as many as the U.S. Census Bureau projection and 10 times the current level, according to a study recently released by the University of Southern California and the National Institutes of Health. Moreover, by the year 2040, when most members of the baby boom generation have entered their elder years, the number of Americans older than 65 may catapult to 87 million, or a quarter of the population. This 87 million figure is 20 million higher than the current census estimate.

According to the new projections, published in the Millbank Memorial Fund Quarterly, one of the country's leading gerontology journals, the average life expectancy of American men could rise by the year 2040 to 87 years—17 years longer than the current average and 11 years more than the census projection.

> At the beginning of this century, a man could expect to live to be 46 years old and a woman could live to be 48. By 1990, those numbers had jumped to 72 years for men and 79 years for women. Bernice Neugarten, Ph.D., 76 year old University of Chicago gerontologist, recently said, "People are living much longer than ever before and in general the quality of life is much better. We have made enormous strides!"

These statistics show some of the realities of our world today. They give us information we need in order to establish opinions and beliefs about our lives, our living, and our dying. The statistical data confirms the probability of our living longer and having more time to use, enjoy, grow with, and to explore lives that will go on long after we stop working. In other words, most of us will retire! And we won't die when we stop working! So, we face the challenge of making decisions now about what we want this gift of extra time to be like. Not only for ourselves, but also for the sake of others in this world who might be able to benefit from what we have to offer through all the things we have learned. Our job now is to clean off the window so we can look ahead and see the beauty and the excitement of that extra time and opportunity. And it is an opportunity! You will be able to explore areas of your life you've never been able to explore before! YOU have some exciting times ahead of you!

The Center for Retirement Success

The programs that are offered through the Center for Retirement Success reflect beliefs and ideas based on information and statistics from this current generation and time. Since the early 1930's, our life cycle has been given a gift of at least 30 years! Retirement is now a fact of life! A reality that all of us have to deal with and manage. For most of us it means 10, 20 or even 30 years of life that is less structured and demanding than any other time of our lives. Most of us will be in good health the majority of those years and we will have better financial resources than any generation before us. We have been highly trained and are motivated to use our skills and training in worthwhile and productive ways.

We Are the Pioneers

We are sensitive people too! We have ideas, dreams, hopes and concerns for those who live now and those who will come after us. We are the pioneers that will be leading our children and their children into a whole new era of life. We will be writing the maps and charting the directions they will follow in the development of their attitudes and hopes for this segment of life. It is important that we view this phase of our lives as a time for LIVING, not just existing. It is essential that we get ready and equipped to live as fully as we can in these years. We want to look through windows that see opportunities, new experiences, and bold new ventures! We want more personal freedom! And, perhaps above all, we want a strong identity as contributing, involved and valuable members of society.

Is this too much to hope for? We do not think so. Is it too hard to see happening? Not at all. By understanding yourself more fully and being willing to work with your own personal expectations and behaviors in life, it is all very probable. The information you gather right now as you read this book will help. You will replace some old messages and beliefs with new ones! Don't you agree that it is time to update some of those old beliefs and ideas? Turning in those outdated and false expectations about life and retirement can really be fun! We believe it will lead you to heights of living you have never before achieved!

Multiple Retirements

In recent times, and particularly with corporate downsizing (or rightsizing), a new phenomenon has emerged .... multiple retirements, or retiring more than one time. Military folks have addressed this idea for years. They would retire from active military service and then begin a new career elsewhere. They would then retire again at the completion of this second career.

It's common now for folks to have multiple careers, and hence multiple retirements. Since pension vesting became law, one can take their retirement benefits with them. This gives us an entirely new vision of retirement; it takes away the notion of finitude, or ending, from retirement and gives it a new, more flexible sense.

The Department of Labor categorizes a person as retired when she or he ....

1. Has a portion of their income from a pension, or pension-like vehicle, and
2. They work less than full time.

As you can see retirement does not mean "the end." Much more accurately, it signifies a clear new beginning.

❖ Introduction ❖

How Do I Get Started?

Todd's Story

Todd Johnson was 60 years old! He couldn't believe it! He could still remember being a kid and going to his grandparents and relatives for visits. Sometimes he'd even think to himself: "These people are old! They must be in their 50's!" He could, in fact, still remember hearing about people who were in their 40's, or 50's, and thinking to himself how old that was. And now, here he was himself, 60 years old!

What did that mean exactly, being 60? It was kind of a funny feeling. Todd didn't actually "feel" different. Oh, some things were different than they were 10 or 20 years ago. He noticed little things. Just this morning he had found it necessary to bend over to pick up something from the floor and felt that sharp reminder that his body just didn't work like it once did. His knees, or maybe it was in his legs, he wasn't sure; anyway, something just didn't work quite the same. He felt awkward! Yes, that was it. He felt awkward, and he had always been well coordinated and quite agile! Todd usually tried not to think much about it because in the back of his mind it made him nervous. It gnawed away at this growing sense he had that he was changing; that he was aging! But, was he really getting "old"?

Todd had a lot of energy! He worked hard! Work was always very important to him. It was fun, it wasn't really "Work" work. It was more a way of life. In fact, it was really his reason for life! He enjoyed his sales position. He liked people and was good at his work. Through the years he had made some long standing friendships and he took pride in the fact that he knew lots of people, met people easily, and got along with most of them quite well. Why, he was better at his work in some ways now than he had ever been! His sales were as high or higher than most of the other sales persons in his company. He still maintained a full and active prospect file that he worked regularly. He was doing everything he had always done. But it was feeling different somehow. Todd couldn't be sure if this funny feeling was something he picked up from other people, or if it was all in his head. Maybe he was getting paranoid; you know, feeling other people were talking about him or looking at him funny when actually they weren't. Lately he would inadvertently catch their eye turned towards him.

What had really started all this was that conversation he'd had with Betty Alverez a few months ago. Betty was retiring in a few weeks. But Betty was 63 and her circumstances were different than his. Her husband had been retired for five or six years already and it was natural that she'd want to leave a bit early and spend time with him. In fact, people seemed to expect if from her! THAT'S IT! Maybe that was what was gnawing at Todd. Do you suppose other people were expecting him to retire now that he had turned 60? Todd had never really considered retiring in a serious way. He certainly knew it was in the cards someday because he contributed to a pension plan, social security and had some private investments of his own. But that was for the future, when he was OLD.

Still, that was how HE saw himself. Did other people see him differently? Maybe as someone who should be retiring? If they did, that really bothered him. That was stress, and that could be what was producing all this uneasiness within him. How was a person supposed to feel and act at age 60? Was he getting too old to be working like this? If other people thought he was too old, how did this affect his ability to do his job even if he did feel robust and full of life? For the first time in his life Todd began to feel old! Maybe he should think of retiring. But how could he even begin to consider all that? He needed to think about this one. Maybe he even needed to get some other ideas or advice from someone. How could he ever really know if he was prepared to make such an important decision in his life?

Alicia's Panic

Alicia was in a real quandary! "Panic" or "depression" were words that might more closely describe her feelings. Jack was insisting that she quit working to spend more time with him. Jack was 67 and had been retired for 3 years already. But Alicia was only 56!

This was her second marriage. After her first husband died when she was only 37, she had raised the two boys and finished college and finally, at age 46, re-entered the work force as an accountant. She liked her job. She felt important and needed. More than that, she felt she had developed an identity for herself, on her own merit, and she didn't think she could just give that up and settle for being a retired housewife.

But Jack was adamant! He knew, from a purely economic standpoint, they could live comfortably without her salary. What Alicia needed was some way, or some per-

son, to help her show Jack why it was so important for her to continue working. Certainly he knew that if she was happy and felt good about herself, she could and would contribute much more to their relationship than if she had to stay at home and adopt a retirement lifestyle that she just didn't feel ready for. Alicia needed help! Where could she get it? How could she convince Jack that she wasn't ready to retire?

Jim's Mistake

Jim had made a mistake. It may have been a very bad one. He still didn't totally understand how it had happened except now he at least knew how badly he felt and how out of control he seemed. Lately he found himself getting up in the morning and having no idea what his plan for the day might be. He somehow seemed to be getting through each day, but when he thought about the years ahead of him, it was almost too much. He was just too young to be going through this.

Jim was 61 years old. He'd been retired now for 4 years as the result of an "early out" retirement window his company had offered. It had been too good to turn down—then. He had received a package deal of benefits, salary plus that all had seemed so good he couldn't have turned it down. Now in retrospect, if he'd just had a couple of months to think it over and some way to evaluate his readiness to make such a decision, he would have done it much differently. But, at the time, everyone else seemed to be doing it and they kept telling him how great it was going to be for him. Some of his friends were still telling him what a great decision it had been for them!

Well, it wasn't turning out that way for Jim. In fact, he was so depressed he was beginning to feel desperate. That certainly wasn't good for his high blood pressure. His physician was already talking to him about doing something to take care of his mental wellness and physical health. But what could he do? Should he go back to work? Should he try and find some kind of hobby?

What really scared Jim was that he still didn't feel as if he understood what had gone wrong. He couldn't seem to get a handle on his problem. If he could just figure out what he was up against, he could get it straightened out. Somehow he had to get himself organized again. He just wasn't ready to sit on the sidelines and watch the others play and enjoy life. But how could he get some control over his life again?

Todd, Alicia and Jim are pretty typical Americans trying to find their way through one of life's most significant transitions. Life transitions, as many of us already know, can be full of surprises and new experiences. This is just the way life is! Because it is this way, it's difficult to know exactly how to do something that has never been done before. These scenarios of Todd, Alicia and Jim are typical of many persons who reach a point of change or transition only to find themselves filled with uncertainty and confusion.

You may identify a bit with one or more of them, and think that your life is very similar. Or, you may be a person who has it all figured out already and has no worries or anxieties at all. Whatever your situation in life may be, you'd probably like to be more confident, more secure, more certain than you are at this given moment that your retirement transition will be accomplished at the right time and in the best possible way. After all, your future life and your next anticipated 25 or more years of living are what we are talking about. If there is a means by which one can possibly increase the chances of these years providing more happiness, greater security and fewer mistakes, wouldn't you like to do it? Of course you would! It only makes sense! This book is written for you and every other person like you, who are concerned and want to make the best decision possible for their future.

As you read along, you'll want to have your Retirement Success Profile (RSP) handy. Your RSP Personal Interpretation Booklet displays your views of the 15 factors which determine overall success in retirement. The RSP doesn't tell you when to retire, nor even if you should or shouldn't. What it does do is give you a clear and precise overview of your personal retirement data. The best decisions are made with the best data. The RSP is unquestionably recognized as the best personal retirement data you can get.

❖ Chapter One ❖
Work Disengagement

Definition: *The degree to which you have distanced or detached yourself from taking your personal identity (sense of self-worth) from your work.*

Each of us draws our definition of who we are from the various activities of our lives. In addition, we were all taught as children what were the most important things . . . what to value and what to discount. Our parents, teachers, friends, acquaintances, etc., all provided models of behavior and thinking which we adopted, to a greater or lesser degree, as part of ourselves. We incorporated what we liked in the world into ourselves and rejected what we didn't like.

Our culture reveres work. It is through working that most of us achieve a sense of identity, productivity, usefulness, purpose, pride and achievement. Work occupies a center-stage position as we play out the drama of our lives, attempting to meet our needs and to express our uniqueness. We have been told in so many ways that work is good. Adages such as "idle hands are the devil's workshop" and "you can tell a person by his fruits" have reinforced the value we place in work. At a very basic level we believe that work is good and if we work well . . . then we are good. Conversely, if we don't work or if we do poor work, we find it hard to think highly of ourselves.

Each of us has been "endowed" with varying levels of a "work ethic," i.e., the need to do well in the world of work so we can feel good about ourselves. We call this "identification with work." Those with a high identification register a strong need to excel at work in order to feel good about who and what they are, while those with low work identification, in large measure, draw their self-esteem from activities or relationships outside of work.

Persons with high work identification place a great importance on their work, their time and their conversation. Even their thoughts are heavily weighted toward their work. Work gives them a high level of self-definition. They wear their work like a badge, constantly flashing it wherever they go. Work is not simply central in their lives, it is of top priority: coming before even family, friends, religion and play. In extreme cases, work becomes their whole life. They feel they are indispensable to the organization for which they work. All their activities, relationships, etc., focus directly or indirectly on their work. This calamity befalls the professional, managerial, and entrepreneurial ranks most often, but no occupations are spared the compulsive concentration on work that this can bring. Our success-oriented culture spawns rank after rank of such folks who march on to ever greater levels of work achievement. It can become highly addictive because their achievements are considerable and are normally rewarded with promotions, raises and ever higher levels of responsibility—which motivate them to focus their lives even more keenly on their work.

Walter

Walter's father was an architect who contracted a terminal illness in the Great Depression years of the 1930's, leaving 9 year old Walter and his mother alone and without income. It was he and his mom against the "cold, cruel and quite economically-depressed world." Walter learned well how to "make a buck" hustling newspapers on the street corner. With great sacrifice and abundant courage, he managed to graduate as a professional architect and almost immediately started his own firm. He worked, and worked, and worked, always fearing the financial collapse of his "empire," even though by every objective measure he and his firm were both thriving. Walter centered his life on his work; in a way, his work was his life.

Helen and Frank

Helen and her husband Frank had raised four children. They were all doing well on their own and had also produced eight healthy, happy grandchildren. Helen had returned to working full-time outside the home ten years ago when her youngest was 14 years old. She received two promotions in the insurance company where she was now quite well respected as an efficient office manager of twenty workers. Her company liked her and she was pleased with the company.

Frank was eligible to retire in 1 1/2 years from the plant where he had worked for almost 29 years. He was looking forward to his retirement and had rather an elaborate plan which included lots of traveling. Naturally he wanted Helen along, but lately was finding himself becoming quite irritated with her as she consistently changed the subject whenever he brought up specific retirement plans.

Relationship to Retirement

The very process of retirement requires that you detach or disengage yourself from your job. Even in those cases where you can go back as a consultant or to some flex-time job-sharing program or other work setting, there comes a day when you have to clean out your desk or work space and leave.

Actually, the disengagement process first begins when the possibility of retirement shifts in your mind and becomes a real probability. You begin to actually consider retirement in more serious, concrete terms. Prior to this shift, which normally happens between ages 45 and 50, retirement is not considered seriously or given clear definition as to a life path. After the shift occurs, however, your thoughts begin forming on how it will be in retirement. If you have a positive attitude toward retirement, your thoughts can be pleasant. If you have a negative attitude, you'll try to avoid thoughts about retirement because they'll be less than pleasant.

The retirement disengagement process is not unique. All of us have had to disengage from one life stage in order to enter another. You could not enter childhood while still a baby; adolescence required you to leave childhood behind and adulthood wanted no part of adolescence. You were forced to move away from one stage with its characteristic ways of behaving and reacting, before you could fully enter the next stage. This process is not always a smooth one; there are bumps and detours along the road. Nonetheless, the growth goes on, sometimes painfully, sometimes with glee, but always with a slight sense of loss that one stage must be "cashed-in" as it were, before the next one can be tackled. So it is with retirement. Before you can enter the new retirement stage, whatever you conceive that to be, you must first disengage from your full-time active work stage.

Projection for Success in Retirement

A word of caution here; disengagement does not in any way imply that your level of productivity nosedives as you disengage. Nothing could be further from the truth. Studies have found that your productivity may actually increase as you prepare for your next career stage by disengaging. Disengagement is an internal process where you begin to take less and less of your "definition of self" from work and thereby shift the sense of who you are away from work and onto other areas. This shift is subtle, intimate and imperceptible. Neither your co-workers nor your supervisor can detect that it's happening.

If a change in your behavior for the worse is noticed, chances are it is not your disengaging that they see, but probably your emotional response to the loss of work, causing a slight feeling of being "down," "sad," or "blue." On the other hand, you could just as readily show a sense of delight, lightness, and brightness, demonstrating that you are happy to be growing and developing. (Note: See Chapter 15 for further discussion on this point.) Persons who are further along in the disengagement process will be ready to retire sooner rather than later. They will look forward to their retirement date, ready to tackle new life tasks.

How disengaged would you like to be before you retire? How much of a shift away from work as a measure of your self-worth would you like to achieve before you take the retirement plunge? This may not be easy because you really have never experienced work disengagement before. You might want to think back if you can to other life transitions where you had to close one door of life before you could open another. Would you like to be 30% disengaged, 50%, 80%, or higher, before you retire?

Walter had some special barriers which were preventing him from fully disengaging at age 63 the way he wanted to. First, his very strong work ethic had always pushed him to excel at work. He felt better when he was working, planning, executing, projecting, estimating and managing. He felt at his best and most confident when he was working. Feeling as he did, it was very difficult to "cash in his self-esteem chips" to enter an unknown lifestyle where he was unsure how he could keep up his self-confidence. Second, Walter had founded his firm; it was his "baby." It was very difficult to hand over the reigns of the firm to any other hands. Third, disengaging from work to enter retirement translated in his mind to . . . aging. Walter didn't want to get old before his time, so a good way to avoid aging was simply to continue working.

These three issues worked against Walter in his attempts to disengage. Sometimes he experienced great internal turmoil and tension between the strong forces working to keep him engaged "on-the-job" and those working to free him from his pressurized work environment; the forces that would allow him to begin a new lifestyle with vigor.

Do you remember Helen and Frank? Helen finally had to tell Frank that she would prefer to remain working for the foreseeable future rather than enter retirement. She wanted to disengage from work when the time came. Her problem was that this was not the time! She almost felt guilty that she liked her job as much as she did. She felt confident, secure and "in-charge" on the job. Helen's work was exciting and stimulating for her. At the office, she felt organized and highly regarded. She liked these feelings and was hard-pressed to give them up. After all, she had only been in the labor force for 10 years and she felt like she could work for a long time to come.

On the other hand, Frank was ready to retire! He had begun his disengagement process years earlier and by now he was counting the days! Frank and Helen had some serious talking to do and some decisions to make. It was helpful for them to be able to see in concrete terms the differences in their attitudes, differences they both knew were there.

Other retirement success factors which are related to work disengagement and which you might want to check out in conjunction with your scores here are:

- Factor 2 – Attitude Toward Retirement
- Factor 7 – Projected Life Satisfaction
- Factor 9 – Leisure Interests
- Factor 10 – Adaptability
- Factor 13 – Familial & Relationship Issues
- Factor 15 – Replacement of Work Functions

Strategies for Change

If you feel it's time to raise your work disengagement readiness, perhaps you would like to try some of the following:

1. Plan for another career after "work."

Investing yourself in a second or even third career after your first retirement is not uncommon at all. Retirement, in its most traditional sense of permanent "rest and relaxation" is not for everyone. You may need more time to take on a full-time retirement. Beginning a second career may be any of a number of options. It could be another job, or it could be starting that small business you always dreamed about. Whatever you decide, try to make this second (or third) career a very personal one in the sense that you decide upon it and you direct it. It needs to be a cause . . . your cause . . ., something into which you can invest your total self.

2. Go back to school/college/university.

Attending school is full-time work. Study is stimulating and growth producing. It opens new options and allows you to think about yourself and the world in new ways. Attending classes forces you to interact with folks of all ages and walks of life. You will grow, expand and enrich your life.

3. Take up an avocational career.

The flip side of the vocational coin is the avocational side. An avocation is an occupation pursued for the pure enjoyment of it. Your chosen avocation may be demanding and even pressured, but instead of becoming distressed by this, you seem to thrive on it because the purpose or goal you are pursuing is so important to you. Such a goal may be social justice or peace, equality, justice, freedom, etc. You are addressing some of the ills of the world over which you could only shake your head in your younger years. Now you have the time and perhaps the financial stability to address them and perhaps even bring about change.

On the other hand, your avocation may be something you do just because you like the process. Activities like painting, crafts of all sorts, gardening, fishing, traveling, etc., can all be pursued for the ultimate joy of the activity and for no other reason. The essential ingredient in any avocational pursuit is that you have a goal! Here you are doing whatever you want (and, by the way, anything can be an avocation) because you genuinely want to do it! (See Chapter 9, Leisure Interests, for a thorough discussion of this point.)

Some retirees stop themselves from doing things they had always wanted because just when they have the time to do it, they judge themselves to be too old. This is pure nonsense; age is truly a subjective measure. The same age is certainly not the same for all persons: 65 is not 65 is not 65! If age is an attitude, then so is youth . . . so develop the youth attitudes in you and forget about the age attitudes!

Suggested Resources

Bosse, Raymond, Aldwin, Carolyn M., Levenson, Michael R. and Workman-Daniels, Kathryn, "How Stressful is Retirement? Findings From the Normative Aging Study," *Journals of Gerontology*, Jan. 1991, Vol.46, No.1, p.P9.

Bradford, Leland P. and Martha I., *Retirement: Coping With Emotional Upheavals.* Chicago: Nelson-Hall, 1979.

Bridges, William, *Transitions.* Reading, Mass.: Addison-Wesley, 1980.

Chapman, Elwood N., *Comfort Zones.* Los Altos, CA: Crisp Publications, 1987.

Elder, G. H., and Pavalko, E. K., "Work Careers in Men's Later Years—Transitions, Trajectories, and Historical Change," *Journals of Gerontology*, July 1993, Vol. 48, No. 4, p. 180.

Erikson, Erik H., Erikson, Joan M., and Kivnick, Helen Q., *Vital Involvement in Old Age.* New York: W.W. Norton & Co., 1986.

Gould, Roger L., *Transformations: Growth and Change in Adult Life.* New York: Simon & Schuster, 1978.

Gradman, Theodore Joseph, *Does Work Make the Man: Masculine Identity and Work Identity During the Transition to Retirement.* Santa Monica, CA: Rand Corporation, 1990.

Hochman, Gloria, "Workaholic's Guide to a Successful Retirement," *New Choices for Retirement Living*, April 1993, Vol. 33, No. 1, p. 42.

LaRock, Seymour, "Neither Federal 'Carrot' nor 'Stick' Alters Early Retirement Patterns," *Employee Benefit Plan Review*, July 1993, Vol. 48, No. 1, p. 10.

Levinson, D. J., *The Seasons of a Man's Life*. New York: Knopf, 1978.

Neugarten, B. L. (Ed.), *Middle Age and Aging*. Chicago: University of Chicago Press, 1968.

Ozawa, Martha N. and Law, Simon Wai-on, "Reported Reasons for Retirement: A Study of Recently Retired Workers," *Journal of Aging and Social Policy*, 1992, Vol. 4, No. 3–4, p. 35.

Robinson, Bryan, *Work Additions*. Deerfield Beach, FL: Health Concerns, Inc., 1989.

Sheehy, G., *Passages: Predictable Crises of Adult Life*. New York: Bantam Books, 1976.

Willing, Jules Z., *The Reality of Retirement*. New York: William Morrow & Co., 1981.

Audio-Visual Resources

Tracy, Brian, *Creative Job Search*. Nightingale-Conant Corp., PO Box 845, Morton Grove, IL 60053-9921 (PH: 1 (800) 525-9000).

❖ Chapter Two ❖
Attitude Toward Retirement

Definition: *Your perception of what your next life stage will be like for you once you leave your current job.*

Have you ever asked, "What ever happened to ________? Is he/she still working at the same job?" Of course you have. In fact, you have probably asked that question many times. We're curious about people we have known and worked with. And usually, when we have received an answer to our inquiry, we draw quick conclusions about what our friend's life may now be like—based on our own impressions of what life will be like—after work.

The attitude you have now regarding retirement has been formed from many different sources of information and observations. Most of us do some reading about retirement. Even reading an occasional article on retirement is enough to reveal the revolution in thinking we are currently undergoing. Until very recently, we have lived with the real handicap of believing that aging was equated with being less valuable. Only now is this concept beginning to be challenged and slowly but surely changed. We all have had some experience within our families, watching parents or grandparents retire and move through their life cycle. Their experiences have been powerful in shaping expectations of what retirement will be like.

We need to remember that it is only in the last two generations that we have had the experience of watching people retire and thereby gain from their experiences. That really is not a lot of time, particularly since we live in a world that changes dramatically with each generation. We do live in a different world from the world our parents and grandparents lived in. Consider the following:

a. Longevity – People are living longer and expecting 10, 20, even 30 years of retirement living.
b. More financial security – Since the 1930's, with the advent of Social Security and personal financial planning, we are better financially prepared to retire.
c. Emotional confidence – We have now had several generations from whom to learn how to retire – so we feel we know more about why we are planning.
d. Retirement no longer represents a simple termination of one's working years. Now it's being approached by people as:

   - A dynamic transition – retiring TO rather than FROM.
   - An opportunity for growing and enriching lifestyles.
   - A time for activities that promote physical, emotional, and social health.

   Rather than:

   - A luxury enjoyed by only a few fortunate persons.
   - Enforced idleness that one accepts without choice.
   - A time reserved for those "too old or weak to work, but too young to die."

Aren't you glad we live in an age where these possibilities and expectations exist? We have choices now about our retirement lifestyles and plans.

In the past 10 years or so, it would appear that an absolute explosion of new energy has been directed toward this issue of attitude toward retirement. We have gone from pessimism to optimism! As a nation, we are living longer, we are living healthier life styles and we are far more productive. Cancer research is hopeful, Alzheimer's is being understood finally, and we are beginning to believe scientists who tell us our brains never atrophy and die! Seventy and eighty year old athletes are competing at levels of performance never before imagined! The whole field of aging seems overflowing with promise and potential. Now we have choices! But, it is these choices that even now inject uncertainty and sometimes turmoil into our lives.

Bill and Margery

Consider the retirement plans of Bill and Margery. Bill worked as an underwriter for 35 years. In the same company! He went to work in the same building and followed the same general life pattern throughout his work career. He was ready for a change! He wanted to travel, to do some reading, and in general find out about all the things he felt he had missed out on because of a rather confining work career. He was anticipating retirement as a time of great opportunity!

Margery had worked part-time as a travel agent for the last fourteen years. She liked working. In fact, ever since the kids had gotten through school, Bill had been wanting her to quit so they could have more time together. She refused. She had watched her father retire and leave his job. He had run out of things to do in three months and lapsed into a terrible depression. He felt isolated, lonely and unimportant. He died within seven months after he retired. Margery had no interest herself in retiring and certainly did not want to encourage Bill to retire. Bill had absolutely no hobbies. What would either one of them do? They needed to stay where they were!

Does that sound familiar? These attitudes/expectations of Bill and Margery represent the extremes of common expectations held toward retirement. Perhaps you have a sense of where your expectations would fall on the spectrum that Bill and Margery present? Factor Two is designed to tell you what kind of expectations toward retirement you do have.

Relationship to Retirement

Your attitude may have more direct application to retirement than any of the 15 factors. If you BELIEVE that retirement will be boring, awful and depressing, you are quite apt to find it that way! Your thoughts about retirement have tremendous effects on your life experience. If you BELIEVE that retirement will be challenging and rewarding, and that it will open new and exciting areas of life to explore, the chances of retirement being just this are greatly increased! For some people, retirement means a kind of "shut-down," and often feels like you have been rejected by the world. For others, it means the kind of experience that "revs up the motors" and stimulates the imagination. What you believe and the expectations you hold about retirement can determine your retirement experience.

Thoughts are like powerful magnets, pulling your life toward them. If you do not like where your thoughts are pulling you right now, this is the time to change your thinking. Changing your thoughts could then quite likely alter your life direction. Remember, you may be traveling this path for the next 25 years! Most of us, given the choice, would prefer a stroll through a rose garden rather than pushing our way through a patch of thistles. We have to remember that we have great control and can choose the path we walk.

Take a moment now to examine where your scores show you to be in your attitudinal preparation for retirement. Think about both your expectations and present behavior scores for this factor.

Projection for Success in Retirement

If your PB score is quite high, it means that you currently have a very favorable outlook on the retirement phase of your life; you see it as a time of promise and fulfillment. You will, in fact, probably want to retire sooner rather than later because you already are convinced that activities other than work will provide your self-esteem needs. You probably have already prepared, or certainly will be doing so, for your retirement. Your retirement will quite likely be exciting!

On the other hand, if your PB score is on the low side, it means that you may have a rather negative outlook on your retirement. Retirement probably feels confining and limiting to you. You may even hesitate to think of yourself leaving "work" because that is where you feel important and useful. You will probably postpone retirement as long as possible and do little in the way of retirement preparation. Eventually, your retirement could quite literally become what you feared!

If your scores fall in the mid-range, it means that you can identify and understand tendencies in both of the extreme groups. Having this information now means that you have the opportunity to make better decisions about the retirement expectations that will have such impact on your future life experience! In what way do you want your life to be influenced?

In our experience, positive (high scores) values convert into high success, and negative attitudes translate into low retirement success. Again, Factor 2 does not stand isolated from the other Profile scores. Other factors to consider in connection with Factor 2 are:

- Factor 7 – Projected Life Satisfaction
- Factor 9 – Leisure Interests
- Factor 15 – Replacement of Work Functions

All the above factors have a direct bearing on this area of your Profile and must be considered as a cluster group. Each of these areas influence your expectations. Consequently, any change or alteration in one of these areas has a corresponding influence in other areas as well. If, for example, you had a very positive score in Factor 2, but very low scores in Factors 7, 9 and 15, you could only surmise that your euphoria about retirement would be very short-lived, because it is based on a very unstable foundation. When these areas all reveal strong, steady scores, the message clearly points toward retirement success.

Think for a moment of persons you know who recently retired and seem to have very positive, strong attitudes toward retirement. A number of examples may come to mind from the lives of persons you have known who were able to maintain very positive attitudes toward their retirement years.

Clarence Pickard

Let me introduce you to Clarence Pickard. Clarence always considered himself to be just a common person. Perhaps it was because of this very quality that his life became an inspiration and beacon of hope. In 1973, John Karras and Donald Kaul, writers for The Register, a Des Moines, Iowa, newspaper, came up with an idea to promote both the state of Iowa and the cause of physical fitness. They decided to organize a bicycle ride across the state of Iowa, border to border, from the Mississippi to the Missouri rivers. Their plan was to start riding and invite anyone who wanted to make the trip to come along. They expected to do the 500 mile trip in seven days. What they did was to begin a tradition that exists to this day and has become one of the most spectacular and well-known bicycle trips in America.

The first year began with about 350 participants. People just showed up with their bikes and said, "Let's go!" One of those riders was Clarence Pickard, an 83 year old retired farmer and teacher who had once earned a Master's degree in Agronomy from Iowa State University and then spent his life farming 160 acres. With little biking experience, but with an enthusiasm and determination to explore life, Clarence Pickard rode every mile of that trip and many subsequent trips across the state. He became rather a legend and an inspiration to thousands of per-

sons who never dreamed they could accomplish a feat such as riding a bicycle across the entire state in just seven days! From a beginning RAGBRAI (Register's Annual Great Bicycle Ride Across Iowa) of 350 members, it grew to 10 to 15 thousand through the years, and today riders represent every state and many foreign countries. The growth was due, in part, to people like Clarence Pickard. Clarence, of course, became a local folk hero, symbolizing the zest and vitality of life available to all people.

> *When his first trip started, Clarence was quoted as saying, "I just thought riding a bicycle across Iowa might be a way of doing some good. I don't know just exactly what good, other than seeing my state and meeting young people." Earlier, while in their 60's, Clarence and his wife Mildred served two years in the Peace Corps, the oldest volunteers ever accepted! Life was meant to be LIVED!, they believed. Retirement was a time to explore and to be adventuresome!*

Clarence illustrates the benefits of an attitude and life style that views retirement in a very positive way. Not everyone has this kind of attitude. Hopefully, everyone reading this book will see value in approaching retirement from this perspective. What may not be as clear is what you can do if your attitude does not reflect this positive approach. If your scores reflect a need for growth or balancing, here are suggestions that will be helpful.

Strategies for Change

If your scores are low, or there is a large variance between your E (EXPECTATIONS SCORE) and your PB (PRESENT BEHAVIORS) score:

1. Set some very specific goals to accomplish in your retirement.

If you have not traveled much and traveling sounds like fun, plan a trip that can be accomplished in the first year of your retirement. Don't make it hard. Keep it attainable so you have a success this first time around. Then, select two or three ideas that interest you and have been part of your thinking for at least several years. Try them out sometime within the first four months of your retirement to see if any of them are "keepers." Also, make a list of projects to do within the next six months, and projects to do within the next three years. Post them where they can be seen regularly. Remember, your immediate goal is to change your behavioral patterns a bit so that your attitude toward retirement will become more positive. Challenge yourself! It's worth it!

2. Seek out people who seem to enjoy their own retirement and get ideas from them.

A friend of ours used to say quite simply, "Stick with the ones who are well!" What she was trying to say was that it is much easier to find satisfaction and happiness in the company of people who are satisfied and happy! Most people have many of the same experiences as they go through life. Some remain positive and happy, others become negative and cynical about life. Those who are positive and happy seem to have more friends and greater satisfaction. Ask yourself which of your retired relatives you choose to visit. Most people gravitate toward the folks who know how to have fun and are enjoying life now! Ask them questions. Observe their lifestyles. Most importantly, do some things differently in your own life so that you have a variety of experiences from which to choose what is best for you!

3. Find people of various ages and interests—don't limit yourself to being with older people exclusively.

Again, consider this illustration from the bike ride across Iowa. Every year in Iowa, some eight to ten thousand people participate. The ride takes seven days and covers a distance of 450–500 miles. People of all ages and backgrounds from every state are there as participants. Several years ago, one of the participants was an 87 year old man. He was the subject of numerous interviews from TV and newspaper people who all seemed to want to know why he was doing it. His stock answer: "I just like to do what younger people do. It keeps me going and its fun!" People need some contact with persons of all ages. It is stimulating and refreshing.

4. Join action groups/hobby groups/ special interest groups/educational groups.

One of the issues for many people who retire is that they find their life beginning to narrow and they feel "out of the flow" of life around them. It is crucial to remain involved and connected with groups, personal friends and support systems that have been part of your life previously. Without these support systems there is an isolating quality that can set in as one adjusts to this new phase of their life cycle.

We have been given such a unique gift. No one else has exactly the life that has been given to us. Each of us has our own special talent, perspective and contribution that only we can make to life. How exciting to view our journey through this lifetime as an opportunity to get more deeply "in touch" with just exactly who this unique person really is, and then to allow that uniqueness to be expressed in the world. No one else can do that or make those kind of discoveries.

Be careful! Doing these things will affect your attitude. The chances of it elevating your expectations and hopes about your retirement life phase are quite high. You will be considering things you have never done and did not think were possible. Are you ready?

Suggested Resources

Chapman, Elwood N., *Comfort Zones.* Los Altos, CA: Crisp Publications, 1987.

Chapman, Elwood N., *Comfort Zones: Planning Your Future.* Menlo Park, CA: Crisp Publications, 1993.

Erdner, Ruth Ann and Guy, Rebecca F., "Career Identification and Women's Attitudes Toward Retirement," *International Journal of Aging and Human Development*, 1990, Vol. 30, No. 2, p. 129.

Haber, Carole, *Beyond Sixty-Five, the Dilemma of Old Age in America's Past.* Cambridge: Cambridge University Press, 1983.

Mosedale, John, *First Year: A Retirement Journal.* New York, NY: Crown Publishers Random House, 1993.

Neuhaus, Robert, and Neuhaus, Ruby, *Successful Aging.* New York: John Wiley & Sons, 1982.

Reeves, Joy B., "Women in Dual-Career Families and the Challenge of Retirement," *Journal of Women and Aging*, 1990, Vol. 2, No. 2, P. 119.

Retirement Advisors, *Retired in America.* New York, NY: Retirement Advisors, 1993.

Viorst, Judith, *Necessary Losses.* New York: Simon & Schuster, 1986.

Wismer, Romaine, *Words of Wismer. "But I'm Too Young to Retire."* R. Wismer: 1985.

Vaillant, George E., *Adaptation to Life.* Boston: Little, Brown & Co., 1977.

Audio-Visual Resources

Krause, Garrison, *Lifetime Strategies for Personal Effectiveness.* Nightingale-Conant Corp., PO Box 845, Morton Grove, IL 60053-9921 (PH 1 (800) 525-9000).

❖ Chapter Three ❖
Directedness

Definition: *The personal quality which determines how you make the decisions of your life. To what degree do you:*

a. rely upon yourself and your own opinions, or
b. rely upon others and outside factors?

Each of us is continually collecting data about our world through our five senses and our intuition. Likewise we are constantly forced to make decisions about many things in our lives. These decisions range from activities of daily living—What should I wear? Eat? What mode of transportation should I take?, etc.,—to very complex and very relevant decisions, like Who should I befriend? What should I do with my time? How should I approach my marriage? What occupation is best for me? Or, When should I retire?

Directedness is that personal quality which determines how you will make the decisions of your life. Will you depend more on your own perceptions and judgements, or will you depend on the perceptions and judgements of others. Again, these two modes of decision-making occupy opposite ends of a spectrum. Where do you fit on this spectrum? To what degree do you make decisions from within, versus taking advice and direction from others. Your score on factor three gives you important information about this area of your life.

Not long ago a pop song hit the charts. Perhaps you remember the lyrics. The female vocalist told of her boyfriend who went to work each day on a train that took him to his work place downtown. There at work he was a nobody! He was simply the cog in a large organizational wheel. He did his job as he was instructed by his supervisors, didn't really expect much except his paycheck. He was allowed no self-direction in his work; whatever he did was directed from outside himself. All this would change, the song continued, when he stepped off the downtown train and arrived in his element, "UPTOWN." In his chosen environment, UPTOWN, he was no ordinary guy, the vocalist asserted. He was strong, direct, decisive and determined. UPTOWN he was somebody; he was totally self-directed.

One of the reasons this song achieved the wide popularity it did was because so many people feel much the same way this weary, uninvolved and unnoticed working man feels. He lives in one environment where he is basically told what to do, and in a second where he is unquestionably "in charge."

No one is completely self-directed or other-directed—that would be impossible. Commonly, we will be more self-directive about some things and more other-directed about others. Each of us lies somewhere along the spectrum of directedness, sometimes edging closer to one end or the other. This factor of directedness, although a rather stable personality trait, can be rather fluid, at times washing one way, while at other times, washing the other direction.

All of us seem to admire those "in-charge" people. That is, as long as they remain in-charge of their own lives and don't try to take charge of ours. We value our individual freedoms. We want to be the "captain of our own ship," the "master of our own destiny." We idealize the John Wayne figures around us. We can even be disappointed when we find our sports stars don't negotiate their own contracts, as we would like to believe they do, as decisively as they field the ball or throw a punch. No, they let their agents fight over the negotiating table for them. We like individualism, the rugged character who comes in out of the cold, having slain the dragon single-handedly.

Yet, in reality, our modern world isn't like that. There are very few, if any, "Rambos" around. We can make precious few of our decisions without considering outside factors and the opinions and rights of others before we can proceed. The more complex our world becomes, the more we seem compelled to consider the "other guy."

Directedness is a retirement success factor which speaks directly to the sense of being in control over your own life. It is that quality which determines whether you are more influenced or directed by yourself (self-directed) or by others (other-directed). Persons who are more self-directed find it easier to make their own decisions, chart their own course and move undeterred in that direction. Persons who are other-directed find decisions much more difficult. They seem to always need more data before they make their moves. This need for more data goes beyond prudent caution. Other-directed persons will want to consult with more and more people, seeking input which often turns out to be contradictory. They can become paralyzed in their own indecision.

Sometimes persons with very responsible positions in their organizations come up with a rather low score on this factor. Naturally, they're incredulous. "Why is this Factor 3 score so low?" they ask. "I make lots of decisions in my job. That's what I'm paid to do . . . This must be wrong!"

At first we were stumped by this apparent paradox. A responsible position like this must require the skills and talents of a very self-directed individual, we reasoned. After thorough investigation, however, we discovered that many times such an individual had a highly developed competency of "keeping his/her finger on the pulse of the organization," kept his/her "ear to the ground," his/her "finger in the air" to determine which way the wind was blowing. No, they're not the corporate "YES-PEOPLE," rather such folks had risen to their responsible positions because they placed a high value on smooth inter-personal relationships. They were great mediators, counselors, listeners and negotiators, working to keep all parties happy and productive.

Consequently, their skills and competencies for self-direction had been discounted without them even knowing it. They value harmony, cooperation and understanding, while at the same time they abhor anger, tension and interpersonal division. Every organization needs people like this; their value is in their arbitration and reconciliation skills. Sometimes, however, they can become more sensitive to the needs and wants of others than they are sensitive to their own.

Harold and Delores

Harold and his wife Delores lived together in relative peace for 42 years. They raised two children, a boy and a girl, both now grown and married. Harold worked in a newspaper printing plant and had retired six months ago after 35 years at the plant. Harold was probably the most steady and dependable worker in the organization. His co-workers would even kid him. "Harold, you don't need to punch-in, they set the time clock by when you arrive in the morning!" To say that Harold was a creature of habit was an understatement. He had risen to the rank of press supervisor some 15 years ago, but after only 4 months he asked to be placed back in his old job where he was much happier.

If Harold was known for his somewhat unassertive approach to life, his wife Delores was known for just the opposite. Where Harold was laid-back and content to "let the world be," Delores was constantly trying to control as much of it as she could. Actually, Harold's ways were exasperating for Delores. But as long as he went off to work by 6:30 a.m. each morning and didn't arrive home until after 5:00 p.m. each evening, Delores felt she had time to herself. She wasn't reminded about what she considered Harold's total lack of interest in her or any other part of life, save television. It was only when watching TV that Harold really shined.

Relationship to Retirement

Those persons who are more "self- or internally-directed," i.e., rely upon their own attitudes and decisions, will use this personality dimension to help them decide when to retire and to more thoroughly plan for their retirement years. Conversely, those who are more "other- or externally-directed," i.e., they adopt the perceptions and decisions of others over their own, are not as likely to thoroughly plan for retirement and may passively accept the conditions of their life rather than trying to influence them. Such persons tend to be less aware of the planning requirements of retirement and somewhat less able to make the necessary retirement decision in a timely manner. Rather than addressing the issue, they may float in a sea of unexamined uncertainty until another person helps them to clarify the issues and the meaning of each.

Excessively self-directed persons, however, may disregard the assistance that others bring to them. There may be an "is now and ever shall be" quality to their thinking. They may not be as open to other perspectives and ideas as the less self-directed person may be. Some self-directed persons can be stubborn and only act on and for themselves rather than being a bit more mellow and allowing things or persons to "just be."

John

John is a good example of this. He retired just last month but already the signs of discontent are evident in him. He becomes irritable at his wife Nancy, and is increasingly critical not only of her, but almost everyone. Even his adult children have been growing increasingly concerned about their father's tendency to "fly off the handle"!

John was always an opinionated man, quick to register his comments, suggestions or evaluation. His "reputation" in the office evolved over the years away from admiration for his independent thinking and toward an exasperation due to his unwavering nature and critical opinions. In short, John didn't take suggestions very well; his way was always the best way. He could change with the times, but make no mistake about whose word would be last in any discussion. John was hard to approach and hard to talk with. He had refused to participate in any of the retirement preparation programs offered by the com-

pany, dismissing them as irrelevant for his needs. After all, he always knew better!

John is an example of an overly self-directed person who has excluded others and developed an "I can do it better myself! . . . what do you know?" . . . attitude. He had somehow taken the normally positive trait of self-directedness and distorted it into a stumbling block to retirement rather than a springboard fostering a successful retirement.

Our first example, Harold, is the mirror opposite of John and yet neither of them fared well in retirement. Neither of them saw the need for planning their retirement even as much as you would plan a vacation or even a gardening project. The interesting thing is they failed for opposite reasons. Harold never saw the value of planning because he always let everyone else, anyone else, take over his decisions. John, on the other hand, wouldn't plan because he was too arrogant to let someone else's opinions mingle with his own.

Planning for anything requires:

1. Gathering data from many sources,
2. Arranging all this information in the hopper of your mind,
3. Incorporating into your thinking how others may have done this before you, and finally,
4. Making decisions and charting a course.

Harold was blindsided in the planning because he simply deferred decisions to other people, most notably his wife Delores and his supervisor. John precluded himself from planning because he thought his own thoughts were better than anyone else's, thereby denying himself the valuable experience others might have given him. Successful retirement planning requires that you occupy a position on the directedness scale somewhere between Harold and John.

Retirement is one of the few, perhaps the only, life stage that you direct on your own. There are few retirement requirements, expectations or guidelines to direct you in your planning like there are in other life stages. When you were just getting into a career, you were armed with the expectations of your parents and teachers, etc. Now, entering retirement, in a sense getting out of a career, your options are wide open. There are no boundaries or expectations. You are, in fact, on your own! For some it can become a bit scary.

Projection for Retirement Success

In broad terms, the higher your Directedness score, especially on the Present Behaviors Scale, the better chance you have of successfully preparing for your next life phase, however you envision it. Persons with higher directedness scores generally can make a more informed decision as to when the "time is right" for their retirement event. In addition, highly (but not overly) directed persons tend to project into the future and plan their lives more thoroughly than do low directedness scorers. This tendency toward planning is most important for a successful retirement.

Higher scores on the Present Behaviors Scale suggest that you are a person with a high degree of self-motivation and normally make decisions based on your own thoughts. You make decisions easily and, in general, feel in control of your own destiny. Persons scoring in this range take personal responsibility for their own actions and accept the responsibility for their own goal success or failure.

People with lower directedness scores tend to let forces outside themselves influence their decisions. They tend to let company policy, job politics and other job-related issues influence their decisions to a much greater degree than high scorers. In broad terms, those persons who score higher on Factor Three prepare themselves better for retirement and can make the optimal decision when their "time is right." High scoring "self-directors" tend to achieve better success in retirement than those persons who score lower on this factor.

Like all the retirement success factors, directedness should not be viewed alone. Other factors in combination with directedness give you a more complete picture of your overall retirement readiness and a means to understand the meaning of your directedness scores as well. The factors that complement the directedness factor are:

- Factor 1 – Disengagement From Work
- Factor 2 – Attitude Toward Retirement
- Factor 7 – Projected Life Satisfaction
- Factor 9 – Leisure Interests
- Factor 10 – Adaptability
- Factor 15 – Replacement of Work Function

For example, suppose you scored high on directedness, but you also scored high on Factor 1 and low on Factor 9. Such a profile would point to avoidance of retirement rather than being drawn toward retirement. Likewise, a low score in directedness, but high scores on Factors 2, 7, 9 and 15 would translate into a potentially high success in retirement. In addition, a low score on Factor 10 (Adaptability) suggests an opinionated personality who might be less disposed to seeking advice and counsel. Such a person may approach retirement like John in our example above.

You may be wondering what happened to Harold and John after they retired. Harold's wife Delores became so irritated and upset after six months of Harold's retirement that she filed for divorce, even after so many years of marriage. His retirement only increased her resentment of him for forcing her to make all the household and life decisions all along. This pushed her to the breaking point. Harold has now gone to live with his daughter and her husband and allows them to make most decisions for him. Delores has found a job she likes and claims to be happier than ever, although somewhat bitter and pained.

John's wife Nancy continues to cater to her husband's every whim, which is getting harder now that John has become more irritable. Nancy does find herself visiting her friends and children more than she ever had before John's retirement. She also finds herself saying silent prayers that John will "find himself."

Strategies for Change

If you are satisfied with your directedness scores and not interested in changing them, your best retirement strategy is to plan for many structured activities. You probably like order and organization. Developing a planned schedule of events will allow you the kind of life to which you are most accustomed.

On the other hand, if you feel your score needs raising, you might try any or all of the following:

1. Find experiences which help you to take risks.

Support-groups for almost anything from overeaters anonymous to adult children of aging parents provide fertile ground for risk-taking and help to enhance self esteem as well.

2. Enroll in an assertiveness training class.

Such classes teach skills in how to assess your feelings and how to express who you are and what you think and feel so that you can achieve a personal freedom you perhaps never knew was possible.

3. Get experience making decisions.

Start with small decisions, like what you want for breakfast or what book you would like to read. Make a decision and then follow through by taking action. Become aware of making decisions based on what you want, rather than what you believe others want for you or from you. Once you solidify your decision, making gains on small things, gradually work up to larger and larger decisions. You'll notice that over time your decision-making ability will begin to soar and your spirits will not be far behind.

4. Give yourself permission to change your mind.

This could be more important than anything else that you do! One barrier for decision-making is the feeling that whatever decision you make is perpetual. That's not true! In fact, nothing is forever! You can change your mind. Once you give yourself this freedom, you'll be surprised how decisively and easily decisions will come.

5. Learn to listen to yourself.

How does one listen inside? Take a course on meditation, or develop contemplation skills. Learn to listen to your own needs and find ways of translating these into action.

Suggested Resources

Alberti, R. and Emmons, M., *Your Perfect Right*. Impact Publishers, 4th ed., 1982.

Dyer, W.W., *Pulling Your Own Strings*. New York: Thomas Y. Crowell, 1978.

Dyer, W. W., *Your Erroneous Zones*. New York: Avon Books, 1976.

Moore, C. G., *The Career Game*. New York: Ballantine Books, 1976.

Newman, M., and Berkowitz, B., *How To Take Charge of Your Life*. New York: Bantam Books, 1977.

Norris, Joan E., "Why Not Think Carnegie Hall? Working and Retiring Among Older Professionals," *Canadian Journal on Aging*, Summer 1993, Vol. 12, No. 2, p. 182.

Payne, E. Christopher, Robbins, Steven B., and Dougherty, Linda, "Goal Directedness and Older-Adult Adjustment," *Journal of Counseling Psychology*, July 1991, Vol. 38, No. 3, p. 302.

Scholz, N. T., Prince, J. S. and Miller, G. P., *How To Decide: A Guide For Women*. New York: Avon Books, 1978.

Weaver, Peter, *Strategies For The Second Half of Life*. New York: Franklin Watts, 1980.

Audio-Visual Resources

LeBoeuf, Michael, *Getting Results! The Secret to Motivating Yourself and Others*. Nightingale-Conant Corp., PO Box 845, Morton Grove, IL 60053-9921 (PH 1 (800) 525-9000).

❖ Chapter Four ❖
Health Perceptions

Definition: *Your subjective assessment and appraisal of the current condition of your total wellness or lack of it.*

Do you feel well? More importantly, is your health a factor that helps or hinders your doing what you want or need to do? These are very important questions that weigh heavily on your retirement readiness. What you believe about the condition of your health has tremendous influence upon your retirement lifestyle and your overall attitude as you enter this phase of your life. It also has a lot to do with your decision about when to actually retire.

Bill and Bonnie

Bill is 58 years old. He is the president of his own company and every week meets a payroll that includes 17 full-time employees and several part-time persons. He started his company when he was 33 years old and has done everything. He has designed, manufactured, and sold specialized automobile clamps for over 25 years. He has seen his business grow from a basement shop into a remodeled factory that is modern, respectable and thriving. This business has provided a good living for him and his family through these years, even providing a college education for three children. Now it is continuing to provide for the needs of other families as well.

It did not just happen! Bill works hard. There were times when he never arrived home until long after the kids had gone to bed and the supper dishes were put away. But Bill has carved out a niche in the market for his product and the business is solid. In fact, he has just received an offer to sell that would enable him to retire comfortably and not have to work like this any more. It is tempting! Until he considers the alternative. The alternative is staying home with Bonnie.

Bonnie has not been well since their youngest daughter left home. She just doesn't feel good. She never wants to go anywhere, she doesn't want to have people over, she doesn't want to have any fun! And Bill has stopped trying to understand it. In, fact, if the truth were known, he doesn't even believe there is anything wrong with her. She does seem depressed, but Bill assumes she doesn't want help because she never makes an attempt to get it. Now Bill's reaction to this is to just get angry and find more work in the shop, where he prefers spending his time. He is especially angry now, because just when he could sell the business and afford to do things and go places, Bonnie appears to have no interest at all in retiring. He might as well keep working. Retirement isn't going to be any fun!

Bill and Bonnie have problems. Many problems! They have problems with their marriage, they have attitude problems about spending time and their lives with each other, and they have never developed mutual interests of any kind to share. Now, in addition to all this, Bonnie has retreated to a position of being ill. She believes that she is not healthy, even though her physician finds very little evidence supporting this belief.

Anyone can quickly see that health issues are going to have a profound influence on the rest of Bill and Bonnie's future. It probably will not be a healthy influence. What we believe about the condition of our health has enormous influence and control over both our behaviors and physical condition. Some scientists would argue that we are, in fact, what we believe ourselves to be.

Dr. Bernie Siegel, author of the best seller, *Love, Medicine, and Miracles* writes:

> "Other doctors' scientific research and my own day-to-day clinical experience have convinced me that the state of the mind changes the state of the body by working through the central nervous system, the endocrine system, and the immune system. Peace of mind sends the body a 'live' message, while depression, fear, and unresolved conflict give it a 'die' message. Thus, all healing is scientific, even if science can't yet explain exactly how the unexpected "miracles occur." (Page 3)

Lest someone think we are a bit too "one-sided," we should recognize a danger here. There always is a possibility of over-simplifying our health problems, pointing a finger at someone who is ill and saying, "You are just doing this to yourself." This, of course, is wrong. The connection of our mind and body is complicated and not yet fully understood. For now, it is best to simply acknowledge that the connection is a powerful one. The number of devoted husbands and wives who live in apparent good health, only to die shortly after the death of their beloved spouse, attests to the significance of mind over body. So, too, does the retiree who dies within months of leaving work, having failed to find a means of renewal in the fashion we are discussing. Even though the cause may be rooted in the mind, the result is real physical suffering.

Relationship to Retirement

Obviously, this factor relates directly to our success in retirement. It is impossible to separate mind from body; they are too closely connected. If our mind tells us we are healthy and that we can control the over-all condition of our bodies, the likelihood of this being true is infinitely greater. If our mind tells us that we are in poor health, and sickly, the probability of this being true is likewise increased. Medical authorities, counselors, and teachers tell us these things over and over. Sooner or later, we can only conclude that these experts know what they are talking about. We do need to recognize that our belief system does have a direct influence on our retirement planning. If we believe that we are in good health, we will probably continue working or move quickly toward a very active retirement lifestyle. If our mind tells us we are ill and in poor health, we will probably retire quickly and seek a quiet, restful retirement life-style. "Resting" or "getting out of the rat race" will be very attractive options in that case.

For people with disabling disease or accident victims, coming to terms with your limitations is crucial to maximizing your health potential. Once again, you must build hopes, dreams, and goals for the future that will enable you to live a full life in spite of your restrictions.

Projection for Success in Retirement

It will be helpful here to look again at the scores you achieved on Factor 4. What are they telling you about your health perceptions?

Scores with a high degree of alignment and in the upper third of comparative scores will, in all likelihood, have greater potential for success in retirement. Persons achieving scores like this regard themselves as healthy and feel they are practicing good health care behaviors. This translates into positive feelings of being in control and having the ability to govern your life in a way that insures the fulfillment of retirement wishes and plans. Factor 4 is also closely interrelated with these factors:

- Factor 2 – Attitude Toward Retirement
- Factor 5 – Financial Security
- Factor 7 – Projected Life Satisfaction
- Factor 9 – Leisure Interests
- Factor 13 – Familial & Marital Issues
- Factor 15 – Replacement of Work Functions

If this cluster of factor scores tends to be low, you will probably be very reluctant to retire. The reason is simple. If you feel or believe yourself to be healthy, yet these other areas suggest a need for further preparation, you will undoubtedly remain in the work force.

Likewise, if the above mentioned factor scores are, in the majority, found to be higher, you will be more ready to move into retirement because you feel prepared and will be eager to enjoy your retirement years and carry out your retirement plans while you are in good health. Your health, in this instance, is actually a "swing" factor, a motivating force that can push you to retire earlier or later, depending upon your scores on the other factors.

Lower PB scores indicate that your own self-health appraisal is rather poor and that you will probably be encouraged by this to retire earlier, in order to escape the rigors and demands of work that is feeling rather stressful. An E score ranking in the lower third of our statistically determined group would point out a lower priority rating that you currently give this issue in your own life. Health is not an area that you seem, at this time, to devote a lot of time, energy or concern to; other issues take priority. This also means that your health situation is not likely to change unless you somehow modify your belief system. Because health is so critical to long-range planning, this factor deserves your most thorough attention.

Americans are being bombarded with information about aging and health issues. Like it or not, we are learning things that affect the way we take care of our bodies and minds. Consider just a few of the things we have learned that impact our health care thinking:

1. "Most of the decline in physical functioning is caused not by aging but by lack of exercise." William Evans, Ph.D., head of Noll Laboratory for Human Performance Research at Pennsylvania State University.
2. Even our very elderly people, between ages 87 and 97, living in a chronic-care hospital, have been shown to almost triple their muscle strength through a simple exercise program done regularly. Maria A. Fiatarone, M.D., Tufts University.
3. Weight lifting exercises appear to develop muscle tissue regardless of the biological age of the participant. And now even the decline in bone density that

often accompanies aging has been shown to be drastically slowed by certain exercise routines.

4. Do we really become more forgetful and "less smart" as we grow older? Michael Kaplan, M.D., Ph.D., (formerly of the National Institute on Aging and currently working in rehabilitation medicine in Catonsville, Maryland) has shown that certain key parts in the brains of animals replenish themselves at every age, birth to death, whenever the animals are challenged. The supposition is that the same is true for people. USE IT OR LOSE IT appears to have new meaning.

We live in a time when increasing numbers of people are proving that living longer does not mean living with less vitality! In the professional sports arena, we have numerous outstanding examples of this:

a. Nolan Ryan pitching his seventh no-hit game at age 44.
b. George Foreman fighting a creditable 12 round world heavy-weight bout at the age of 42, and not finished yet!
c. Robert Parrish playing center for the Boston Celtics at the age of 40, planning on several more years!
d. Professional golfers playing world class rounds into their 50's and 60's.

Where will it end? One of the really ageless role models of physical fitness in America is Jack LaLanne, living in the hills of Hollywood, California. He has been dazzling our nation for years now with his skin-tight jumpsuits and ballet shoes. He literally crackles with energy and has devoted the last 45 years of his life to promoting physical fitness through TV shows and health clubs around the country. Every year, on his birthday, he has performed some gargantuan feat of endurance to promote the importance of physical fitness. These are some of his more notable accomplishments performed through the years:

1. Age 40 – He swam the two-mile Golden Gate bridge underwater, carrying 140 lbs. of scuba gear in 55 degree water. It took him 45 minutes.
2. Age 41 – He swam over two miles, from Alcatraz to San Francisco's Fisherman's Wharf, wearing handcuffs. When he arrived, he lurched out of the water and did 30 push-ups to further demonstrate his fitness.
3. Age 42 – He performed a world record 1033 push-ups in 23 minutes on the "You Asked For It" TV show.
4. Age 45 – He completed 1,000 push-ups and 1,000 chin-ups in one hour, 23 minutes.
5. Age 60 – He completed a swim from Alcatraz Island to Fisherman's Wharf (again), handcuffed and shackled, towing a 1,000 pound boat.
6. Age 65 – He towed 65 boats filled with 6,500 pounds of wood pulp in Lake Ashinoko, Japan. (People started believing in physical fitness!)
7. Age 66 – He towed 10 boats filled with 77 people over one mile in less than one hour!
8. Age 70 – He towed 70 boats, with 70 people, one and one- half miles in Long Beach Harbor, handcuffed, shackled and fighting strong winds.

Jack LaLanne may even now be planning his next assault on our awareness of the importance of physical fitness in our lives. He believes in miracles! His belief that anything is possible with the human body are reflected in some of his more famous sayings:

> "If the mind can conceive it, the body can achieve it!"
>
> "Man has never cured anything. Doctors have never cured anything. The body cures itself!"
>
> "Would you get your dog up in the morning and give it a cup of coffee, a cigarette and a donut? You bet you wouldn't. You'd kill the damn dog. But think how many people do that every day and wonder why they're sick!"

A vegetarian, nutritionist, physical fitness advocate, Jack LaLanne is a role model for what he preaches. His diet is extremely important, as is exercise in his own life. Following his standard, he says, the following results will be achieved:

> "They're going to feel better, they're going to look better, they're going to live longer, their sex life's going to be better, their brain is going to work better. Everything about them is going to be better. This is fact. This is truth. You don't have to embellish it or con people; you just tell them the truth. Everybody wants to feel better and look better. Everybody wants to improve his sex life. If they don't, they're dead. It all comes down to physical fitness, how much energy you have to give out." (*Fitness Energy Magazine*, Sandra Lerner, June/July, 1988.)

Strategies for Change

Your world and your life in particular can be better if you function with all the energy and creativity available to you. The important thing now is that you begin to believe that this world needs you to find that excitement and zest that comes from living and feeling good! It's there! If you decide to find that excitement again, and to respect yourself more by taking better care of your own health, here are some ideas about how to begin. These are suggested by Kathryn Dawley, R.M., M.A., Associate Professor of Mental Health and Holistic Health at Grand View College in Des Moines, Iowa.

1. Eat good food.

This means, for most people, eating more vegetables (raw or lightly steamed), whole grains, fruits, fish and less red meats. Be sure to eat breakfast and start cutting out sugar, salt, and additives/chemicals from your diet. Start experimenting with herbs and natural flavorings. You'll be amazed at how much better you feel!

2. Exercise regularly.

Start a program based on reliable guidance. Read Ken Cooper's book, *The Aerobic Program For Total Well Being* (1982, but still helpful), or one of the more current editions on the market. Follow carefully the program recommended for your age group and health status. See your physician first if you are over 40 or have any health problems. Many people in our nation have become addicted to the benefits of regular exercise. A colleague has a descriptive phrase that conveys this thought quite well. He says that, at age 59, he jogs not to add years to his life but rather to add life to his years.

3. Sleep seven or eight hours a day.

Your body needs time for rest. You'll find sleep comes more easily with a good diet and exercise program. Less than seven and more than eight hours a day is not healthy and tends to make you excessively tired and weak. Strive for a routine.

4. Keep your weight within ten percent of your ideal body weight.

Avoid drastic dieting. Even more important than weight is body fat composition. Have yours checked and follow the advice to get yours to a healthy level. Eating good food, along with a regular exercise program will combat the majority of weight/fat problems.

5. Do not smoke and if you drink, do so only in moderation.

These practices have been shown to increase the pace of your aging. (If you are chemically dependent, do not drink at all. There are many good treatment programs available for help.)

6. Program your "computer" with positive messages.

Tell yourself, "I am a healthy person." "I am a lovable person." "I have all that I need to accomplish what I want in life." Use whatever messages that you want, or buy a tape and listen to it in your car or whenever you need a lift.

7. Go outdoors at least two hours every day.

John Ott (1973) has completed fascinating research on the importance of the full spectrum of sun light for human health. You do not have to be in the direct sun to benefit. In fact, to avoid burns, go outside in the morning or evening or stay in the shade. It's also a good way to work on your relationship with your environment. This time is well spent in relaxation, exercise, or developing a deeper understanding of your environment.

8. Laugh every day.

Learn to laugh at yourself and spend time with people who laugh. Or just laugh—it does not have to be at anything funny, because the physiological effects are the same. But, don't leave out crying. It is just as important. Some of us have learned to laugh and cry at the same time!

9. Relax.

Learn the relaxation response. Take at least ten minutes out of every day to allow your body to rest and heal. Again, there are many tapes out to help you learn this skill. (But don't do it in the car while you are driving!)

10. Treat all problems/crises as opportunities.

Don't hesitate to take the opportunity to learn more about yourself. Take advantage of counseling, self-help groups, friends, prayer. Treat all illness/symptoms/troubles as a message and learn what they are telling you.

11. Enjoy.

Start any or all of the above slowly, perhaps one at a time. Again, approach them as opportunities to feel great, not things you have to do to live longer, or it won't work.

Suggested Resources

Cousins, Norman, *Anatomy of an Illness as Perceived by the Patient.* New York: Norton, 1979.

Dardik, Irving and Waitley, Denis, *Quantum Fitness.* New York: Simon & Schuster, 1984.

Glassman, Judith, *The Career Survivors;And How They Did It.* New York: Doubleday, 1983.

Hallowell, Christopher, *Growing Old, Staying Young.* New York: William Morrow, 1985.

Pelletier, Kenneth R., *Longevity; Fulfilling Our Biological Potential.* New York: Delacorte Press, 1981.

Pelletier, Kenneth R., *Mind As Healer, Mind As Slayer.* New York: Delta, 1977.

Shealey, C. Norman, *The Pain Game.* Berkeley, CA: Celestial Arts, 1976.

Shealey, C. Norman, *Ninety Days to Self Health.* New York: Bantam Books, 1980.

Siegel, Bernie S., *Love, Medicine and Miracles.* New York: Harper & Row, 1986.

Toughill, E., Mason, D. J., Beck, T. L., and Christopher, M. A., "Health, Income and Post-Retirement Employment of Older Adults," *Public Health Nursing*, June 1993, Vol. 10, No. 2, p. 100.

Audio-Visual Resources

Stone, Robert B., *Mind/Body Communications: The Secrets of Total Wellness.* Nightingale-Conant Corp., PO Box 845, Morton Grove, IL 60053-9921 (PH 1 (800) 525-9000).

❖ Chapter Five ❖
Projected Financial Security and Planning

Definition: *Your appraisal of the degree to which you have accomplished the necessary planning to sustain adequate financial security so you can maintain your desired lifestyle during your retirement years.*

Financial security is a condition that seems to be universally sought; i.e., everyone seems to want it. Our society, with its capital-driven economy gives high priority to wealth measured in dollars. We seek to acquire the goods and services which money can buy not simply because we need them, but often because we want them. Our economy, in order to run smoothly, demands that people spend well beyond their necessities and expend ever increasing amounts of what is called "discretionary income," i.e. money you are able to devote to non-necessities.

Money is important to us, not simply for its buying power but because we tend to equate our personal worth as an individual with our bank account. We therefore don't necessarily desire goods and services for acquisition's sake alone but because we seek to enhance our status in the community. You've heard the saying about money being the best way of keeping score in the "game of life"!

Very few of us seem satisfied with our current level of assets . . . we always seem in quest of more. I recently heard an interview with a self-made person who made a fortune in the fast-food business. He mentioned that his first goal was to become a millionaire. After he made his million, he developed a new goal . . . one hundred million! He had achieved even this goal and had now set a new goal of one billion dollars. It was also interesting to hear him say, by his own admission, that he probably wouldn't live any better as a billionaire than he did as a millionaire! So why do we aspire to reach ever higher levels of income? Maybe you could say we do it for the simple pleasure of doing it! Money does motivate! It doesn't motivate everyone in the same intense way and certainly we know that other factors like recognition, fame and adulation play major roles, but money still pushes us on.

Harry

Harry has always wanted financial independence. As a salesman for a major company, he comes in contact with large corporate cultures everyday and has developed a love-hate relationship with them. He loves the challenge of closing a sale and giving quality service to his customers. On the other hand, he hates the politics and "meat grinder" mentality which seems at times to view people as expendable. Harry dislikes the fact that the careers of some of his friends in the company could come crashing down at the apparent whim of the "higher-ups." For this reason, he has always fantasized about his own business. Some years earlier he had even taken some steps to start his own manufacturer's rep.'s organization, but somehow the dream seems to have faded. Now, at the age of 58, he welcomes his retirement from the steel company so he can start his own enterprise. He has his idea, and now all that he needs is some financing to set his fledgling organization on a steady track.

His wife Harriet knows Harry is anticipating retirement and his new enterprise but reminds him of their lack of retirement savings. Harry and Harriet had put four children through college, had always vacationed, drove fairly new cars, and liked to socialize. There always seemed to be more demanding places to use their coveted funds than placing them in IRA's, TSA's or other investment and savings programs for retirement. Consequently, Harriet wants to hold on to whatever assets they do have, rather than risk them in Harry's new business. She knows how much this means to Harry, but it is just too great a risk for them to take.

Income in retirement comes from three basic sources:

1. social security
2. pension plans
3. personal savings & investments.

A general rule of thumb is that it will require between 65–75% of your preretirement income to maintain a similar standard of living after you retire. The problem retirees face, of course, is uncertainty. No one has a crystal ball to predict the rise in the inflation rate. Nor can one project financial resources required for unforeseen events such as accidents and health care. Not to mention the unpredictability of your length of life. The medical community has devised many, many ways they can use to keep your body going, much longer than your parents or grandparents.

Relationship to Retirement

The simple fact is that you don't know how much money will be necessary for your retirement years. What is adequate? Retirement could be the longest stage of your life, lasting 20, 30, or even 40 years. With uncertainty such as this, only the most well-heeled individuals can be certain of sufficiency. Yet there are ways, often found through the help of a financial planner, that retirement income can be assured; but it does require planning.

Money is generally considered the keystone of retirement preparation. Unquestionably, financial security exerts powerful direct and indirect influence on your retirement timing decision and your eventual retirement success. However, money alone cannot "purchase" retirement success. Certainly, financial solvency can buffer any life transition and ease the sting of unfortunate events in your life. However, the importance of money can be overemphasized to the point where you come to unwisely believe that retirement preparation and financial sufficiency are synonymous; i.e. retirement planning and financial planning are one and the same. Such is not the case, however. Finances are very, very important for success in retirement, but they are not the entire "ball-of-wax." There are 14 other factors which must also be considered before you can say you have a complete picture, a comprehensive profile of your eventual success in retirement.

Nonetheless, financial security is one of two premier factors, the other being perception of health (Factor 4). It therefore deserves much attention. Almost every other factor is related to some measure or degree to either finances or health. Indeed, finances and health are closely related to each other. However, it's interesting to note that the actual level of dollars available for retirement is not the criterion of interest here. Rather, it is your own subjective evaluation of the sufficiency of your financial planning for retirement which is the fulcrum upon which your financial peace-of-mind balances. You may have ample money available to you in retirement, but if you believe you need more, the chances of your retiring earlier rather than later are very slim.

It should also be noted that of all the 15 retirement success factors, this area of financial planning is the most changeable or volatile. Your assessment on this factor can change faster and farther than on any of the other 14. Your score of today could only slightly resemble the score you might achieve if you evaluated yourself in three months. Your actual dollars invested may not have changed in those three months, but your perception of the adequacy of those same dollars could change dramatically! How can this happen? We really don't know the answer to that question. Perhaps your perception changes with the monthly rise and fall of the leading economic indicators . . . we simply don't know!

Projection for Success in Retirement

Persons who score high on the E-scale (Expectations Scale), and in fact most people do, really want to plan well for their retirement. They know that they should plan and not leave it to Social Security to do it all for them. Social Security was not designed to be a full replacement for income lost after you retire. The unfortunate part here is that good intentions do not fill your bank account!

The higher you score on the PB-scale (Present Behaviors Scale), the higher your satisfaction with your financial planning to date. You are to be congratulated that you probably have established an adequate financial base which should serve you well in the future. Because of this readiness, the chances are that you register a willingness to retire sooner rather than later. Of course, you must look at some other retirement factors to generate the most accurate assessment of your retirement timing readiness. Specifically, these factors are:

- Factor 1 – Work Disengagement
- Factor 2 – Attitude Toward Retirement
- Factor 4 – Health Perception
- Factor 7 – Projected Life Satisfaction
- Factor 10 – Adaptability
- Factor 11 – Identification With Past Life Stages
- Factor 15 – Replacement of Functions of Work

If each of these factors points in the higher rather than lower direction, we can conclude that your readiness to retire is quite high. On the other hand, if several of them point in a lower direction, and especially if you scored very low in one of these factors, then in all probability your readiness to retire now or in the near future requires a second look. Please see "Strategies For Change" below.

If you scored lower on the PB-scale of financial planning, this means that you feel your financial preparation to be inadequate at this time. You probably experience increased concern about your financial position and, in all likelihood, register a reluctance or fear of retirement, even though you may wish to retire. This factor, because of its central position in the total scheme of retirement planning, can present a real barrier for you in your quest for retirement success.

Phil

Phil wants a great retirement! So many times in his younger years he would think about the wonderful freedom of action he would have when he retired. Now, at age 55, he is faced with a stark reality. After 19 years with his corporation, they are offering him a retirement window. He will receive a generous severance/retirement package, including health benefits and a monetary bridge to age 62, when Social Security would "kick in." It sounds good to Phil; in fact, many of his friends in the company are more than happy to accept the plan.

Phil is hesitant. He found out, to his surprise, that most of those who were accepting the plan had been participating in the company savings plan all along. Some have IRA's and other investments to lean on in their retirement years. Phil has none of this. "How is it," he asks himself, "that they have all these savings and I don't? They didn't make any more money than I did! Where did it all go?"

Phil is struck between the eyes! He doesn't have the options that he sees his friends enjoying. What about those pleasant thoughts of retirement he had dreamed about? If Phil took the retirement window package, he would be forced to go right back out into the labor market and undertake a job search. Even though the package contains provisions for an outplacement counseling firm, Phil feels very timid about undertaking a job search campaign at his age. He also feels he can't match his salary anywhere else. For the first time in his life, he feels trapped and very frustrated, if not somewhat afraid that he no longer has the necessary time to construct a retirement savings plan to meet his needs later on.

Barbara

Barbara is an emergency room physician and has worked in the same hospital for 20 years. She has stayed at the hospital because she is comfortable with the health care and value system encouraged there. All along she has participated in the 401 K plan, a tax-sheltered annuity where an amount was withdrawn from her check each month and placed in an investment vehicle of her choice. Now, at age 55, Barbara feels she does have options; she could move to a less demanding position if she wanted. She has been fully vested in the hospital pension plan for some time now and feels a pleasant level of comfort knowing that even if she did change jobs she would still be financially secure because of the decisions she had made and kept years before. Her plan has worked!

Strategies for Change

Here are several directions you could take or improve upon should you desire to address your financial position.

1. Get accurate information.

The first thing you need is accurate information about your current financial situation. It's surprising to note the number of intelligent people who have only a foggy notion of their financial condition. Gathering data of this sort is best accomplished with professional, objective assistance. In most cases, a financial planner has the tools and the experience to make a comprehensive evaluation of your situation so that he or she can present an array of savings and/or investment possibilities to you. Financial planners receive their income in one of two ways, either by charging a flat fee for the service or through the commissions they receive on the investments they make for you. They usually don't receive income from both. Ask them how they operate before you enter into any agreements.

2. Develop a budget.

Budgets impose the kind of discipline necessary to achieve the goals you want. Both Phil and Harry are examples of what can happen when you don't follow a budget. It's never too late to begin a savings plan. Analyze your position and decide how much of your income is going where. Once you know this and have your budget in front of you, stick to it!

Suggested Resources

Addicott, James W., *Securing Your Future*. San Jose, CA.: Financial Arena, 1988.

Clark, Robert Louis, *Retirement Systems in Japan*. Homewood, IL: Irwin, 1991.

Hallman, V. G. and Rosenbloom, J. S., *Personal Financial Planning*, Third Edition. New York: McGraw Hill, 1982.

Klosowske, Allen, *Personal Financial Fitness*. Los Altos, CA.: Crisp Publications, Inc., 1987.

Simon, Ruth, "How to Retire Early With All the Money You Will Ever Need," *Money*, June 1993, Vol. 22, No. 6, p. 102.

Underwood, Don and Brown, Paul B., *Grow Rich Slowly: The Merrill Lynch Guide to Retirement Planning*. New York, NY: Viking, 1993.

United States Congressional Budget Office, *Baby Boomers in Retirement: An Early Perspective*. Washington, D.C.: Congress of the United States, Congressional Budget Office, Sept. 1993.

Weaver, Peter and Buchanan, Annette, *What To Do With What You've Got*. Glenview, Ill.: Scott, Foresman & Co., AARP Books, 1984.

Young, Arthur and Co., *The Arthur Young Preretirement Planning Book*. New York: John Wiley & Sons, 1985.

Audio-Visual Resources

Gillies, Jerry, *Moneylove: The Power of Prosperity Consciousness*. Nightingale-Conant Corp., PO Box 845, Morton Grove, IL 60053-9921 (PH 1 (800) 525-9000).

❖ Chapter Six ❖
Current Life Satisfaction

Definition: *The degree to which you believe you have achieved contentment and peace at this point in your life.*

In her best-selling book, *Passages*, Gail Sheehy pulled together the theoretical and practical realities of life that people struggle to cope with and understand. Most people who read that book gained enormously from its ideas on adult development and life change. Sheehy reminded us that our lives are continually growing and changing. As long as we have life and breath, we are evolving and moving through one life stage to another, periodically in transition. If we are normal, our lives will never remain the same for very long. Change, growth and new experiences must be incorporated into our lives as we move along. If they aren't, we become developmentally "stuck" at some point in our life journey and may not mature at a normal pace. Unfortunately, this happens too frequently.

The astounding thing is that it does not happen all of the time to all of us. Moving along our life track means constant change. Crisis looms before us every time we go through a transition. Many gerontologists tell us that transitions can last from one to three years. These periodic transitions lead into the next life "stage," a period of time normally lasting from five to seven years. During this time, most persons enjoy a routine that is quite peaceful and in most ways uneventful. Various life cycle scholars and theorists have proposed stages through which all people pass. Elsie Frenkel-Brunswik, a psychologist in Vienna in the 1930's, was the first to write about the definable stages of life that people pass through. Her work pioneered that of Erik Erikson and his great work *Childhood and Society*, 1950. Erikson outlined life as unfolding in very observable sequences, each one marked by a "crisis," defined by Erikson not as a catastrophe, but as a turning point, or a time of "increased vulnerability and heightened potential." (Sheehy, p. 19) Other sociologists and psychologists have since developed our understanding of these life stages even further. Some of the more noted ones include Robert Havighurst, Daniel Levinson and Vivian McCoy.

Corley and Johnson, in their book *Adult Development in the Five Life Arenas*, described these stages and transitions of life:

1.	Leaving home	ages	18–21
2.	Becoming adult		22–27
3.	Age 30 modifications		28–33
4.	Establish adulthood		34–39
5.	Mid-life re-examination		40–45
6.	Re-stabilization		45–50
7.	Age 50 modification		50–55
8.	Preparation for retirement		55–60
9.	Late adult re-examination		60–65
10.	Retirement – new beginnings		65–70
11.	Age 70 modifications		70–75

12. Life Enrichment 75–80
13 Late, late adult re-examination 80–85

It is crucial to understand these developmental stages because they give meaning and perspective to our lives. The transition phases are vital because they provide the linkage or passage way from which we can safely move from one stage to another, leaving behind the issues that must be left behind and embracing the issues that face us in the next stage. Transitions can be upsetting because they involve movement and change. The more obvious transition points people often speak of are:

a. Adolescence – a psychological movement within and away from the dependent family position.
b. Getting married – leaving home and the establishing of one's own routine and system of family life.
c. Mid-life – a time of turmoil and new decisions, exploration and recommitment to a pattern.
d. The "Empty Nest" Phase – when kids leave home and parents have to re-establish relationships with each other; a routine not organized around children.
e. Pre-retirement – a time when careers, personal identity, and family relationships all intensify as change becomes clear.
f. Retirement – the event becomes reality.

There are other transitions along the way as well. It is important they be seen as challenges and opportunities. People who can view changes in this light have a greater chance of moving forward toward their goal of life maturity. Transitions move us toward stages. Stages last longer and are usually more placid, routine and uneventful. These are the times we build, put down roots, develop traditions and establish ourselves. When these issues have been accomplished, we face the next transition . . . and the life cycle continues. Occasionally, it is good to remind ourselves of what we already know. Namely, that until the issues in each stage are dealt with completely and finally, we will not be able to successfully move on to the next stage, or progress toward full maturity:

> "These developmental stages and transitions are not random or haphazard. They occur, rather, in a particular sequence. You cannot die before you are born, parenting comes after childhood, training before work, experience before wisdom, and youth before maturity. Your life structure creates a pattern of development, a path running through your years, developmental stages and transitions. Like pages in a book or seasons of a year, your life progresses in developmental steps, each building on the last one and the one before that. Your present stage of development has less meaning without knowing what came before and some understanding of what will be in the future." (Corley and Johnson, 1979, p. 9)

Relationship to Retirement

Having this perspective on our life stages is directly connected with the understanding of our score in Factor 6. To score well in this factor, we must have successfully mastered the challenges presented to us in the preceding life stages or we will feel conflicted and unable to enjoy a higher degree of life satisfaction. We can too often become overwhelmed with unresolved issues from previous life stages never resolved or mastered. From your own observations, you have noticed some people struggling with these unresolved issues constantly. Our path through life becomes a continuous process then, of assessing our immediate or current level of life satisfaction; checking our pulse, so to speak, seeing if we're happy or unhappy. We do this by gathering information and feelings about ourselves from six life arenas which are constantly influencing and giving form to our lives. In chart form, these six life arenas look like this:

Six Life Arenas

Career Arena	FamilyLife Arena	Relationship Arena
Inner Life Arena	Spiritual Arena	Leisure Time Arena

Perhaps the best way to verbally describe the impact these six life arenas have on our lives is to describe one clear picture that comes to mind. It is the picture of a TV technician sitting in a control booth watching the monitors in front of him. Six different pictures are being viewed simultaneously and his job is to select the one that has the most impact and relevance to the viewer, the one that conveys the most pertinent message at that moment of the program being broadcast. His mind must take in all six images at the same time and filter them through a cognitive process that he believes produces the best picture. Quite a job! But one that we handle in similar fashion all the time! Thankfully, we make our decisions from what we feel and experience from only six sources of input, those six life arenas that merge in and out of our minds with differing degrees of influence all day long.

Let's look quickly at each of these six arenas.

1. Your "career" arena.

This arena encompasses your work and day-to-day activities in life. It includes everything you do, think about, plan for and worry about connected with your work—getting to and from work, short term goals and long term goals, salary negotiations, office parties, friendships and conflicts at the office. How many times a day does your work occupy your mind? For some, it is constant, for others seldom. Everyone must deal with messages from this life arena because we all have roles we perform in our career arena even if our life work is not a paid job.

2. Your "family" arena.

Families are with us forever. We begin our life journey in a family and we usually leave this life from the midst of a family. During that journey, we play many roles, moving from infant, to adolescent, to young adult, adult, and elderly adult. Along the way, we are sons, daughters, parents, aunts, uncles, grandparents and friends. We learn our traditions, establish our identities and develop our values from these experiences. They continually influence us. How do you balance and control the thoughts that flood your mind every day in this life arena?

3. Your "relationships" arena.

We have many relationships with different people that involve us in varying levels of intimacy. Our relationship with the mechanic at the service station is different from the relationship we have with our spouse/significant other. Intimacy is defined as sharing ourselves. It is found in all of our relationships, but is measured according to the level and quality of sharing given to each. Those relationships we value most usually receive our deeper sharing of thoughts, feelings, commitments and time. Mental health professionals tell us we all need several persons in our life with whom we can share deeply. If we don't have those people, we may have stress. How is this area of your life?

4. Your "self-life" arena.

This is the "intra-personal" area of your life! This is where you relate to your inner "self"—feelings, thoughts, ideas, beliefs, and values. Have you made peace with yourself? Do you like who you are? Do you respect your own values, ideas and beliefs? Do you realize that your inner-life is totally connected to the way you feel, think, and live?

The "self-life" arena actually has two distinct components. The first is our internal self relationship. This includes such issues as self-esteem, feelings about ourselves, self-confidence, an internal sense of stability or turmoil, self-control, self-discipline, and self-regard. While each of these overlaps a bit, all of them speak to an internal sense of self-understanding.

The second part of "self-life" is your relationship with your own body. What is your body image? Do you like your body? . . . . respect it? . . . . cherish it? . . . . worship it? What about your relationship with your body parts? Your head? . . . . hair? . . . . toes? . . . . ears? . . . . heart? . . . . kidneys?, etc. All of this is part of your "inner life." Your inner-life is totally connected to the way you feel and live! It spills over and determines how you feel and your own personal level of "wellness"! Kathryn Dawley, R.M., M.A., writes:

> "First, start by thinking of wellness as the integration of body, mind and spirit, and the appreciation that everything you do, think, feel, and believe has an impact on your state of health. Most of us tend to dwell on the body, i.e., exercise and diet, when we think about wellness. And, they certainly are important, but I would like you to think of 'Wellness' as harmony of body, mind and spirit in an ever-changing environment. When these three are in balance, we experience wellness. Illness indicates an imbalance."

5. Your "spiritual life" arena.

There is a relationship here with a higher power, whatever you conceive that to be. As people mature, there is a progressive and normal desire to find spiritual comfort and meaning in their lives. These kinds of existential questions are most easily entertained in times of quiet reflection. For some people this means deep involvement in a church or synagogue and real effort to be open to a personal relationship with God. For others it means cultivating a purpose in life, or a sense of an ultimate meaning that becomes clearer in one's living. Others discover values and a belief system that points them forward with renewed hope and spiritual integrity. How do you feel about your "spiritual" arena? It is an important part of your total life response. Is it balanced in your life?

6. Your "leisure time" arena.

This is the sixth, but certainly not the least important of your life arenas. Here you are in charge. This is where you refresh your spirit and renew your body. Here you find some of your deepest enjoyment because you do what you need for self-fulfillment and personal enjoyment. Whenever you do what you want to do, when you want to do it, in the way it is most pleasant for you, you are involved in cultivating your leisure time arena. And it is so enriching! This is where you have FUN! This is where the child, sometimes buried deeply within you from too much work and too many "adult" responsibilities, comes leaping out for fresh air and stimulation. You need to have fun, to relax and to play. Many people never learned to have fun, or have become so caught up in a rigorous work ethic that they no longer give themselves this time. It is a huge mistake to not cultivate this area of your life. Since you already know you are going to have many years to live with your feelings about this area of your life, why not do what is necessary to bring it into better balance? Your life will be more exciting and fulfilling.

These are the sources of information you draw from, then, when you respond to someone who asks you the simple question, "Hey, how's it going? How are you feeling about your life today?"

Your answer reflects that quick assessment made by your own mental computer (your mind) as you evaluate where you are with experiences gleaned from those six life arenas. Hopefully, as you approach retirement, you can respond with a high degree of satisfaction. A note of encouragement: Our research shows that if you are satisfied with your life now, there is good indication that you will be satisfied with your life in retirement.

Look at the scores you achieved on this factor. Again, the first score you see is your Expectations score and the second line is your Present Behaviors score. As you look at them, check the size of the Variance and where it is placed on page 22 of your Interpretive Report. This will tell you if you have achieved a level of life satisfaction you can be comfortable with. If not, this quite probably will carry over into retirement, making your overall adjustment more difficult.

Retirement planners formerly believed that if a person was happy in his work, he would not want to risk a change by retiring; he would continue working instead. As more data has been gathered and assessed, we are discovering that a person satisfied and content as a pre-retiree will quite likely be a satisfied and content retiree because he/she has already learned how to adjust and live successfully under changing conditions. Again, what we learn from our research is that people become more unique and individualized as they get older. For example, some people, if they are unhappy with their current life, will be more inclined to retire. Others find their life has always been unsatisfying and they have no reason to expect that to change by retiring. These people would not be influenced toward or away from retirement because they know their retirement will be just as discontent as their life has been thus far.

Finally, we know that high scores of current life satisfaction will keep some persons from making changes in their lives. Others, who believe strongly in their ability to achieve satisfaction anywhere, will approach retirement with little hesitation.

Projection for Success in Retirement

How do the scores you achieve on this factor relate to your retirement decision? Higher scores reflect a satisfaction with the six arenas of your current life. Most persons who score high also put forth great effort to make sure there is a proper balance in these areas of their life and place a high priority on a lifestyle that demonstrates all of these components. Those with high scores believe it is important to be satisfied with life. That belief is so important for most of them that they will usually not permit events, circumstances, or other people in their lives to prevent that goal from being achieved! Usually, they will not stay long in relationships that are not contributing to that goal!

Lower scores reflect a general dissatisfaction with your personal level of fulfillment. This may translate itself behaviorally into a rather depressed, negative, disinterested attitude toward life. There is little motivation to put energy or time into any of the six life arenas. Low scores here are red flags pointing the way toward a need to make necessary changes now in your life.

Factor 6 (Current Life Satisfaction) should be considered with scores on Factor 7 (Projected Life Satisfaction). If Factor 6 indicates you are dissatisfied with your current life, and scores on Factor 7 support this, you will be reluctant to retire. If Factor 7 scores were high, you might have a tendency to rush toward retirement as a way out of an unhappy time of life. If both Factors 6 and 7 are low, it could reflect feelings of such discouragement and depression that making any kind of decision to change your life will be difficult or impossible to achieve. Other factors that have a direct relationship to Factor 6 are:

- Factor 5 – Financial Security
- Factor 12 – Dependents
- Factor 14 – Perception of Age

These factors influence each other and should be considered as a cluster.

Norman

Norman's counselor is not happy with him. Norman is certainly not happy with his counselor either! In fact, he had not wanted to talk to this person. It was not his idea. Norman is angry! He is angry at himself, at this counselor who does not seem to be doing anything, and at his family who pushed him into this place and told him he had to get help. He did not think he should be here.

Norman is 64. He has been retired now for almost a year. So far, he is not happy or content. In fact, he's bored, disappointed and angry. But, he had sometimes felt that way when he was working, too. He probably should not have retired. His company had offered him this chance to leave early and he had taken it. Maybe he could have thought it through more carefully, but he had not done so. He was not happy where he was. Why not try something else?

When he was still working, Norman had taken some kind of test designed to show him if he was prepared for retirement. He had not scored very high on parts of it and the answer that came back to him was that he needed to make changes before he made this decision to retire. Maybe he should have listened. The test had shown that he was not happy and that he was really expecting to have great things happen after he retired. His test interpretation had also said that was not likely to happen because he was not prepared well enough in other areas of his life either. Well, he did not want to listen then and he does not want to listen to this counselor he is sitting with now, either!

Norman is not someone many of us want to adopt as a role model. As one looks ahead, Norman's life doesn't appear very attractive. Most people with a profile like Norman's would be wanting to make adjustments or corrections so they could have a happier future. We're glad to report that Norman is a minority. But what can be done if one decides they want to increase their level of current life satisfaction?

Strategies for Change

1. Take another look at the six life arenas.

On a piece of paper, write the six life arenas across the top of the page. Then list under them things that you can relate to in each of these areas. This could be something you like or don't like; something you feel good about or something you feel uncomfortable with. You might put down specific ideas, or even people who come to mind as you consider each of these arenas of your life. Whatever the idea, thought or area of concern, write it out on a piece of paper or write it here in your book. It could look something like this.

Career	Family	Intimacy	Self-Life	Spiritual	Leisure
1.	1.	1.	1.	1.	1.
2.	2.	2.	2.	2.	2.
3.	3.	3.	3.	3.	3.
4.	4.	4.	4.	4.	4.
5.	5.	5.	5.	5.	5.

Put down the negative things as well as the positive things. What you're after is a realistic appraisal of how you feel currently about each of these areas in your life. Are you satisfied or are you discontent? Is that true in all six arenas or only for one or two?

Obviously, you need to begin to focus on where the discontent in your life is coming from. Once you know this, you can begin to make changes that will bring you a greater sense of satisfaction. If, for example, you find that you have a long list of items under the life arena of "work," you may have to do some careful sorting of items on that list. Again, if you have 12 more years to work before you can retire, and you list nothing but frustrations and problems under your life arena of "work," a change in your working career may be in order. After all, 12 years is a long time to look ahead to being unhappy! Do not give up and let yourself believe that you have no options. It may be difficult to change jobs or careers, but it is not impossible. If you are giving yourself a strong message about being unhappy in any of the life arenas, you need to do something about it.

Follow the same procedure with the other life arenas. **Identify where your frustration is coming from!** Then do something about it! Here are some further suggestions you may want to consider.

2. Explore what spirituality means to you.

a. Join a church.
b. Get involved in a spiritual renewal center.
c. Find a growth group/support group/reading group.

3. Invest time and energy in yourself. You're worth it.

a. Enroll in self enrichment programs in an adult education forum.
b. Find out what really gives you pleasure in life/leisure interest counseling.
c. Join a committee in your favorite organization to learn more about having/being a friend.
d. Do for someone what you would like a friend to do for you at least once every week.

You have a right to be happy! You also have a responsibility to know what it is you need in order to be happy! Understanding your six life arenas can provide invaluable information to you, enabling you to strengthen areas of your life needing adjustment.

Suggested Resources

Alberti, R., and Emmons, M., *Your Perfect Right*. New York: Impact Publishers, 4th Edition, 1982.

Anderson, Chalon E., and Weber, Joseph A., "Preretirement Planning and Perceptions of Satisfaction Among Retirees," *Educational Gerontology*, Jul-Aug 1993, Vol. 19, No. 5, p. 397.

Corley, J., and Johnson, R. P., *Adult Development in the Five Life Arenas*. Gainesville, FL: University of Florida, 1979.

Helmstetter, Shad, *What To Say When You Talk To Yourself*. New York: Grindle Press, 1986.

Kaufman, B. N., *To Love Is To Be Happy With*. Fawcett Press, 1977.

Lemsky, Carolyn, "Assessing Retirement Satisfaction and Perceptions of Retirement Experiences," *Psychology and Aging*, Dec 1992, Vol. 7, No. 4, p. 609.

Levinson, D. J., *The Seasons of a Man's Life*. New York: Knopf, 1978.

Audio-Visual Resources

Finley, Guy, *The Secret of Letting Go*. Nightingale-Conant Corp., PO Box 845, Morton Grove, IL 60053-9921 (PH 1 (800) 525-9000).

❖ Chapter Seven ❖
Projected Life Satisfaction

Definition: *The degree to which you look forward to personal success, achievement, contentment and peace in the future years of your retirement stage of life.*

The notion of life satisfaction at first blush sounds like a very passive idea; it kind of makes you want to yell, "I don't want to be simply satisfied, I want to really LIVE!" It seems to speak of only surviving when you actually want to thrive. However, life satisfaction, especially when applied to the future can be the most uplifting and life sparking notion there is. Projected Life Satisfaction includes goals, successes, motivation and that marvelous sense of internal contentment we call "peace-of-mind."

Ray

Ray worked as a camera technician at a downtown TV studio. He had grown up with the station as a matter of fact. He opened their doors back in the 50's when he was only 20 years old. Now, at age 63, he was going to retire in only one month. We ran into him in the hall at the studio when we were there to give an interview. Since our topic was retirement and Ray was about to retire, the station manager introduced us, thinking we had something in common, which of course we did. In retrospect, perhaps she realized that Ray needed help.

After we exchanged greetings, we asked Ray what he had planned for his retirement. His immediate, and standard response was, "Oh, I'm going fishing." Right then we realized that Ray had a problem. We had talked to too many folks ready to retire who had similar responses to this question, only to see them "crash" three to six months after they retired. We knew by now that you can only go fishing everyday for just so long before it begins to wear thin.

Ray had, upon closer questioning, a very positive view of retirement. He really thought that fishing would take up the majority of his time. Ray hadn't been fishing for the last six months; from the sound of it, his world seemed monopolized by his work at the studio. The more we talked, the more convinced we became that, even though Ray verbalized a positive life for himself in the future, this seemed merely lip-service to the deep turmoil inside him which had him so confused and scared that he was trying to fool himself. In reality, his projected life satisfaction was anything but high.

How you view your future plays a dramatic role in the decisions you make today. Today is the foundation for tomorrow. The way you see the wind blowing today has a significant impact on how you set your sails today and where you'll end up tomorrow! When your future appears to be a time of growth, a time when you expect to achieve success and satisfaction in living, then the present will tend to be a calm and contented time as well. When you feel like this, your natural fear of the future is greatly diminished and the future beckons us closer.

In the last chapter, Current Life Satisfaction, we introduced the six life arenas. You got the opportunity to view your life as a spotlight swinging back and forth among the six arenas as the focus of your life shifted and changed. You can use the same notion here with projected life satisfaction.

Goals

When we speak about projections into the future, we are necessarily talking about goals. It may help you appreciate the importance of goals if you imagine yourself driving down a dark country road in your car at night without headlights. Now, we hope you haven't actually had that kind of experience, but even without actually living through it, you can probably relate to what it would be like. Not very well! Goals are like headlights on your car! They pierce the darkness up ahead so you can proceed with confidence. Without goals, you're like a car without headlights. When you have goals, your trepidation goes way down; you're no longer afraid because you have direction and purpose.

So where do you get goals? Goals are your best guesses of where you would like to go with and in your life based upon expectations, past successes and your level of motivation. When you have goals for the future your scores on this factor of projected life satisfaction will swing way up.

Success

What is success to you? What type of successes have you had in your past? What type of successes do you plan in your future? Success means different things to different people. Success is one of those indefinable concepts which can only be described in effective, very personal terms. Success is—a satisfying feeling, a sense of accomplishment, an attitude of completion, the calmness ad confidence of knowing a job was well done. The idea of achievement is at the root of success.

Whether you realize it or not, success has created a pattern in your life. You have certain personality-specific abilities which you seek to use in a very particular manner and mode. These motivated abilities can be identified if you examine yourself. If you can pinpoint the personal abilities you used and how you used them to achieve the successes in your life, then you will be able to guide these motivated abilities to give you new successes in the future. Each of your past successes bears your indelible mark—they didn't just happen—you made them happen. You can discover these personal success trademarks and use them to help you plan successes in your retirement.

Motivation

Success, of course, is an outcome of motivation and action. Motivation is the driving force behind any and all genuine successes. Motivation is as complex as you are. It is the sum total of your needs, desires, values and plans, whether these are conscious (you are aware of them) or unconscious (you are not aware of them). You may have a desire to learn to play golf or tennis, or to write a book, or to start a new business or to create a successful retirement. But in order to accomplish these goals, you must become actively motivated.

Research has shown that motivation has three components:

1. **Achievement motivation:** the tendency to achieve success. How driven are you to get to where you want to go? This trait seems to be unevenly distributed in the population; some people have an abundance, others don't have as much. Achievement motivation can, however, be developed.
2. **Probability of success:** your perception of how likely it is that you will achieve success in any given life arena. When tasks are perceived as having either a very high or a very low probability for success, then the tendency to achieve that success is low. Your tendency to achieve success is more strongly aroused by tasks you perceive as having an intermediate probability of success.
3. **Relative attractiveness of success:** What's in it for me? What are my rewards? This motivation quality is also known as the incentive value.

The kind of motivation so far described is "positive motivation," defined as the tendency to achieve success. There is another type of motivation, however, called "negative motivation," which is defined as the tendency to avoid failure. Rarely can you identify tasks which are clearly either all positively or all negatively motivated. Usually there are elements of both present, creating an internal struggle with every task attempted. One side of you says, "YES, go ahead, do it, succeed." The other side of you says, "NO, don't do it, you may fail." But the failure would be embarrassing personally, so your motivation to perform the task is one of avoiding failure. It is enlightening to identify which motive is strongest in you, the motivation to achieve success or the motivation to avoid failure.

Relationship to Retirement

When you identify the similarities in the successes you achieved thus far in your life, you will be able to engineer your post-retirement activities to almost guarantee future successes. Projections of continued life satisfaction into retirement will necessarily raise your level of readiness to make your next life transition much easier. You can look forward to a continuing source of self-worth and self-esteem in retirement when you can look at the future with a sense of anticipation of good things to come. Perhaps you'll even anticipate experiencing certain things which you have deferred due to work. If you feel this way, you'll be more inclined to retire sooner, all other factors being equal, rather than later.

On the other hand, persons who project a decrease in their ability to achieve personal fulfillment, success and happiness in the future will "back into retirement" with lots of second thoughts, insecurities and fears. There is little incentive and therefore little motivation to change your lifestyle when the future looks devoid of satisfaction.

Frank and Sally

Frank and Sally were both quite active people. That is, until just recently. It seems that Sally's mother, now 79 years old, is demanding more and more of her time. And this change is causing problems. Frank has always been very close to his mother-in-law, but as her dependency increases, he is finding it harder and harder to be around her. This new attitude toward his mother-in-law seems to have produced a negative impact on Frank's normally cheerful demeanor, and especially his projected sense of satisfaction in the future. Formerly, he had always anticipated his retirement as a new and well-deserved life phase, full of opportunities for experiencing things he never had the time for before. Now it seems to Frank that his future is not as bright and promising. His mother-in-law's increasing debilitation has pushed him into thinking that a similar fate could befall him or Sally. He unconsciously avoids that uncomfortable feeling by denying the future. He simply doesn't talk or really even think about the future . . . he is fixated in his present way of life.

Projection for Success in Retirement

How do you see yourself in terms of projected life satisfaction? Do you look forward to a time of expanding horizons and exciting options, or do you think, as some people do, that maturation is simply a slide into old age and senility? Do you have goals? Do you see successes for yourself in the future? To what degree are you motivated? All of these questions are components of your overall projected life satisfaction.

Most people score quite high on the Expectations scale; very few of us want an unsatisfying future life. If you didn't score in a higher range, it might be a good idea to talk over your attitude about your future life to discover what blocks exist for you here, and further, what you might do to modify your attitudes. If you don't project positive things for yourself in the future, chances are you will receive exactly what you expect.

The Present Behaviors scale asks you to evaluate where you are right now with regard to future goals, success and motivation. Persons who score higher on the PB-scale usually have well-formulated goals, plans and expectations about the future. They anticipate more than acceptable alternative activities and have a high interest in moving toward the goals with a positive attitude of successful motivation. Consequently, they feel an enhanced level of present security, knowing the future will provide good things. People who have high scores seem to register a peace-of-mind, a contentment that all is well with them, and therefore have only minimal fear of the future.

Persons who score lower on the PB-scale may exhibit a measurable level of fear about changing their current life-style; they are inclined to stay right where they are. Their present life may have a theme of insecurity running through it as well, because the future is so uncertain. Consequently, they would be more inclined to push off the retirement event due to the unpredictability that lies behind it. They feel more safe and secure where they are and so they want to prolong it as much as they can.

Margaret

Margaret is in somewhat of a dilemma. She scored high on Factor 2 (Attitude Toward Retirement), but rather low on Projected Life Satisfaction. She is perplexed as to how this could be, since most folks who score high on 2 also score high on 7. She likes the idea of retirement. She has seen some of her friends and church members seem to revel in retirement. She looks forward to traveling, reading, community and church service. In short, she has things to do in retirement. So why the low score on projected life satisfaction?

Margaret's family seems to have more than its share of cancer in it. Margaret has seen both of her parents and two aunts die slow and traumatic deaths due to cancer. In the recesses of her mind, Margaret projected that this same fate could befall her. She was afraid, and sad about this at the same time. She did everything she could do now to keep herself healthy and active. Yet, the mental snapshot of her parents and relatives on their deathbeds comes over her like a dark cloud at times. When this happens, she notices her reaction is to concentrate even harder on her work as a direct mail marketing executive. Underneath all her plans, Margaret harbors some unresolved fears about getting older and experiencing a difficult death. She talked to her family doctor about this. He reassured her that her chances of developing cancer were no greater than anyone else's, and that even if she did, new treatment modalities have been developed since her parents' deaths which have enhanced the cure rate dramatically. He also explained the new medications now being used which fantastically reduce the pain and suffering cancer patients experience. This talk greatly reassured Margaret, who is now more confident and able to complete her retirement preparation work.

Strategies for Change

1. Develop goals for your future.

Look at each of your six life arenas and develop at least two long term goals you would like to achieve in each. Under each of your long term goals, list the specific objectives you must tackle on your path to meeting your long term goals. You may find that you need 6 to 12 objectives for each goal. For example, one goal in your self-life arena might be "to become as healthy as I can be." Such a goal requires you to accomplish many, many objectives along the way. These objectives might include very basic decisions, such as forming an exercise program, establishing a proper diet and having regular medical examinations. Each of these objectives can be seen as a building block in your over-all construction of a total wellness program.

2. Recognize the importance of success in your life.

Continue to analyze and develop the areas you seem to call upon again and again to achieve the successes in your life. Successes are no less important for you in retirement than they have been all along, perhaps more so. You are the master director of whether you achieve success in retirement . . . it's all how you define it.

3. Keep yourself motivated.

Attempt to understand the kind of forces which motivate you best. No kind of motivation is bad. The important thing is to keep the stream of motivation flowing. Even negative motivation, that brand of motivation which stems from fear of failure, can be beneficial as long as you "keep the luster." You want to maintain your verve and vitality! These qualities know no age boundaries.

4. Develop a plan for inner-peace.

Peace-of-mind is our most basic goal, success and motivation. Without peace-of-mind, we wander in a frenzied circle of confusion without the vital value underpinnings so necessary for focused action and genuine satisfaction. It's not simply performing the activity, but knowing "why" you are performing the activity which enhances the meaning, purpose and the sense of positive after-glow you receive from any action.

5. Reconcile any conflicted relationships now.

Nothing can sabotage a potentially successful retirement more than harboring bitterness, resentment and distrust toward people close to you. Take active steps to reconcile, to bring peace to each conflict. You may find that the other party may not be as enlightened as you; he or she may rebuff you in your attempts to bring about harmony, or at least peace. If this is the case, you have but one recourse . . . detach with forgiveness. It doesn't take two to forgive; it takes only your willingness to do so. Remember, you're forgiving the other party not for his or her sake, but for yours—to free you from the tethers of negative emotion which consistently block you from achieving peace-of-mind.

Suggested Resources

Adair, Suzanne R., and Mowsesian, Richard, "Meanings and Motivations of Learning During Retirement Transition," *Educational Gerontology*, June 1993, Vol. 19, No. 4, p. 317.

Anderson, Chalon E., and Weber, Joseph A., "Preretirement Planning and Perceptions of Satisfaction Among Retirees," *Educational Gerontology*, Jul-Aug 1993, Vol. 19, No. 5, p. 397.

Bach, R., *Illusions*. Dell Press, 1977.

Blythe, Ronald, *Living To Be Old*. Harpers, July, 1979.

De Genova, Mary K., "Reflections of the Past: New Variables Affecting Life Satisfaction in Later Life," *Educational Gerontology*, Apr-May 1993, Vol. 19, No. 3, p. 191.

Deller, John J., *Achieving Agelessness. Retirement Is a New, Exciting Career. Here's How to Make It All It Can Be*. Harbor House West, 1991.

Ferguson, M., *The Aquarian Conspiracy*. T. P. Tarcher, 1980.

Kelly, John R., and Westcott, Glyn, "Ordinary Retirement: Commonalities and Continuity," *International Journal of Aging and Human Development*, 1991, Vol. 32, No. 2, p. 81.

McLeish, John A. B., *The Ulyssean Adult; Creativity in the Middle and Later Years*. Toronto: McGraw-Hill-Ryerson, 1976.

Nouwen, Henri J. M. and Gaffney, Walter J., *Aging*. New York: Doubleday & Co., 1974.

Reis, Myra, and Gold, Dolores Pushkar, "Retirement, Personality, and Life Satisfaction: A Review and Two Models," *Journal of Applied Gerontology*, June 1993, Vol. 12, No. 2, p. 261.

Audio-Visual Resources

Robbins, Anthony, *Unlimited Power.* Nightingale-Conant Corp., PO Box 845, Morton Grove, IL 60053-9921 (PH 1 (800) 525-9000).

❖ Chapter Eight ❖
Life Meaning

Definition: *The degree of purpose and significance you find in your total life experience at the present time.*

Picking up a morning newspaper, looking at a weekly periodical or even listening to the evening news on TV can be a very depressing experience! Events selected as being newsworthy often seem to be the catastrophes, accidents, assaults and moral failures of people around us. Personal triumphs and the achievements necessary just to get through a day don't capture headlines. It seems unfortunate that society has the need to focus its attention so intently on negative happenings. It keeps most of us from ever getting headlines and the attention we deserve for leading solid, dependable, predictable and stable lives. After all, where would the world be if we did not continue doing the things we so routinely do—day after day after day?

But the world *is* this way. Accepting the world on its own terms means we will probably continue to be bombarded with news and daily reminders of every failure, problem, potential disaster, etc., that could ever happen. The really amazing thing is that, in spite of this, many people maintain a spirit of optimism, hopefulness, and trust (faith) in life. They continue to believe that our world has a future, that by working together we can solve our world problems, that people can be trusted, that we can learn to live together peacefully, and that loving people is better than hating them! When you think about it, that is astounding! Most people still believe that life has meaning and purpose! Have you found a meaning and purpose for your life?

Life meaning, as it is defined in Factor 8, refers to the ability to extract sense, spirit and expression from your internal and external environments. In other words, it's an answer to that existential question about whether or not your life really has a meaning and a purpose. Everyone struggles at times with that question. Life meaning can only be measured in terms of your subjective appraisal of some internal sense of wholeness. Life meaning borders on a spiritual concept. Indeed, spirituality and faith in a higher power would certainly be large parts of your overall life meaning. Life meaning, or this factor, refers to your ability to regard your present life as being rich, full and personally fulfilling; not simply that you are meeting your needs, but that there is order, rhyme, reason and a direction to your life. The feeling that your life is a whole unto itself, while at the same time being part of a larger whole, is at the core of the notion of life meaning.

Most people find ways to explain life. As humans, we have a need to explain, or make sense of our experience of living. What is life all about? Do the things we do, and the traditions we enforce and follow really mean anything? Everyone asks these questions in one form or another. The way you answer these questions has a lot to do with your inner and spiritual life. Ask a theologian to explain it and he/she would say it has a lot to do with the doctrine of eschatology, or a study of the future. Religious eschatologists have much in common with the futurists of our day who stress the importance of planning for and thinking about what is yet to happen. Earl Brewer, noted gerontologist, has emphasized the importance of future planning. Among other things, he writes about the debilitating effects the commonly held belief that old people have no future has on the elderly. He stresses that this belief leads quite naturally to the deterioration of an older person's self-image and then to depression as they begin to believe they will be useless in the future.

We think it's quite likely that the self esteem of older people will soon receive a real boost as business and industry begins to address the larger and larger commercial market the elderly present. When older models begin to sell us products and speak to us during TV commercials, it will be a boost to many people! To this point in our history, older people have been too frequently ignored and treated as being unimportant.

It is often at this point in their life cycle that older people really begin to reflect upon their lives. They begin to tell stories and reminisce about past events and times. Most often, this is an attempt to find meaning and purpose through some understanding of what their lives have been all about.

Earl Brewer writes: "Life review for the elderly is not sufficient; they must also engage in a 'life preview'." (Earl Brewer, "The Future of Religion and Aging as Transcending Processes," Futurist 4 (1980): 368–370.) This "life preview" is built on the belief that even though life on a horizontal, or physical, level may have numerous limitations, many elderly persons are simultaneously able to cultivate and develop a vertical or spiritual perceptiveness. This spiritual dimension produces an inner/spiritual caring for the whole world, and enables these individuals to set goals and even assume responsibilities for future relationships. People must always hope and plan for their future! Now is the time to build and strengthen a belief system that affirms your worth and value as a person. First you must believe that having life always means you have hope and personal value.

Many religions espouse views of life after death that certainly influence and inspire a positive concern for immortality. Many sects within the Christian community teach a literal on-going connection of this life with God's offering of eternal life in a world yet to come. The traditional Eastern religions offer an on-going life-cycle of rebirths, whereby individuals progress toward an elevated existence and the world evolves more and more toward a perfect life. Many individuals deal with a need for immortality with direct legacies of information, systems of beliefs, or even tangible structures willed to children, disciples, or progeny of some kind. Whatever our belief system, we must learn how important it is to reinforce and activate this system during our retirement preparation. Establishing and cultivating religious foundations reinforces the conviction that there is meaning and purpose, tasks to accomplish and a reason to live throughout one's lifetime. This message is crucial to our sense of life meaning.

Relationship to Retirement

How does this factor relate to your retirement readiness? Generally, your perception of meaning in life is unique to you. No one else experiences your life quite the way you do. Further, your perception of life's meaning remains more or less stable throughout life. Consequently, the level of life meaning you achieve in these pre-retirement years is a good barometer of the level of life meaning you will experience after you retire, assuming other factors remain constant. Therefore, it can be said that the success you achieve in retirement is influenced to a large degree by the measure of life meaning you have achieved thus far in your life. The importance of this life meaning factor in promoting a decision to retire is somewhat negligible. However, our research is showing that high life meaning scores before retirement are positively correlated with high levels of success in retirement. Again, your objective is to achieve a retirement as rewarding and satisfying as it possibly can be.

Think about this area of your life for a moment. Again, think specifically about your expectations and your current behaviors in this area of your life. As you consider your retirement living, do you believe it's important to have a strong sense of "life meaning"? And, equally as important to consider, are you currently doing the things necessary to enable you to achieve that kind of score? How do you feel about your scores? Remember, changing them is possible.

As you look at your scores, remember that the top line represents your expectations score, that is, the level of life meaning you would like to, or that you expect to achieve before you retire. The bottom line represents your present behaviors, that is, the level of life meaning you believe you have actually achieved to date.

Projection for Success in Retirement

Higher scores on the PB scale indicate that you already enjoy a sense of achievement and have a good deal of pride in your accomplishments. You probably enjoy a sense of doing some things well and have found a sense of peace and fulfillment, being in harmony with all that is around you. You feel in control of your life, which also permits you to trust and permits others to interact with you on a level that encourages sharing and understanding. Retirement will probably be very satisfying for you because you have gained a perspective and faith that permits you to see beyond the immediate issues around you.

If your scores are lower on the PB scale, it probably is an indication that, at this time in your life, you are not feeling a significant level of achievement or purpose. Having this level of dissatisfaction in your life means it is also difficult to establish and maintain a faith or belief system that can nurture or encourage a spiritual growth or awareness. Because the level of meaning that you currently find in life tends to be carried over into retirement, your score indicates some attention to this area is in order. Unless you are content to live in retirement feeling as you do, or even more discontent, you need to consider ways to raise your score. Perhaps your biggest challenge will be to change your mindset to one that will permit you to allow change or to believe that you can change.

Naturally, as you move toward retirement, you may move back and forth a bit in terms of your life satisfaction. As you mature and consider more fully the implications of retirement, it will be very important to pay close attention to the issues that draw you to high levels of life satisfaction. That is certainly where your greatest potential for satisfaction lies.

Persons with high scores tend to view retirement positively, as they have most likely viewed other phases of their lives. They can do this because they have in some measure learned to transcend life a bit, having found values and beliefs that stabilize their personal lives, even while their environment may be quite shaky. If you are one of these people, retirement will not be as big an issue for you because life already has meaning for you. Regardless of what you do in your retirement, your overall life meaning will probably not be affected. On the other side, however, those who score lower may seek some kind of meaning or purpose in retirement that they have been unable to find in their working careers. If you are one of these people, you may be drawn sooner to retire in the hopes that you may find greater fulfillment in life. Sad to say, without some definite alterations in life and attitude, you may be disappointed again.

Jimmy Carter

Consider two very well known persons who illustrate this transcendent ability in life. The first is a former president of the United States, Jimmy Carter. Jimmy Carter, of course, served as the President of the United States of America from 1977–1981. Historians are still writing and analyzing the effectiveness and effects of his tenure in office. He and his wife Rosalyn brought a Southern influence into the White House that had not been there before. They also brought a Baptist faith tradition to America's attention and confronted a religious sensitivity that had not been confronted this way before. America suddenly began hearing about their President leading the men's Bible class in his home town church of Plains, Georgia. Then they had to make a decision about whether or not a man could be religious and still be President! It put many people in a terrible dilemma between their intellect and their belief systems. But somehow, through all the turmoil and religious bickering, President Carter was able to focus an entire nation's sensitivity on matters of conscience and issues of integrity.

President Carter began his tenure in office with a heritage of Vietnam and Watergate, both terribly divisive events in our nation's history. These watershed events cast large shadows over the oval office where he worked. America had been torn apart by deep feelings of moral conflict over the war and equally deep feelings of sadness, disillusionment and despair over Watergate. Trust in government and its elected leadership was very low. Our nation's morale and belief in itself was equally low. Jimmy Carter became the president of a nation that had all but lost faith in itself! Carter's challenge was to not allow himself to lose faith in the nation!

The next four years of his political life were extremely stressful. His strong convictions about the needs for strengthened civil rights legislation and world peace brought him much stress and conflict. He worked long and diligently on these issues throughout his term in office. In 1980, he faced perhaps his greatest challenge when he negotiated for the release of the hostages in Iran. Much of his work and most of his ideas never saw completion. His presidential defeat in 1980 was decisive and terribly disappointing to him and his staff and his family. He had fully expected to have another four years in office to complete his agenda and purpose.

At a moment of defeat such as this, one is sorely tested. Jimmy Carter had lived his life with a belief and religious faith that permitted him to carry out his duties in office and to then move on to the life of a retired president. Life did not lose its purpose or meaning, despite his intensely personal setback and political defeat. These later years have seen him working steadfastly in the areas of civil rights, world peace, and human need. He regularly participates, with other people of his faith group, in a mission committed to re-building low-income housing for needy families, called Habitat for Humanity. Certainly it was obvious to those around him, that his faith and belief system sustained him and enabled him to transcend the impact of those difficult defeats that tumbled into the pathway of his life. His sense and understanding of life's meaning, and, in particular, his own life's meaning, will undoubtedly sustain him as he makes the transition toward his own retirement.

Mother Teresa

Another celebrated person whose life illustrates that transcendent ability to maintain perspective on life because of a belief or faith system is Mother Teresa. Mother Teresa is a Roman Catholic nun who heads the order known as the Missionaries of Charity. Nuns who are members of this order work among the poor and the outcast of almost every nation. Mother Teresa was born in 1910 to Albanian parents. Her family instilled in her a strong sense of family love, an equally strong sense of responsibility for using wealth, and the ability to help and serve those less fortunate. Mother Teresa became totally committed to those values and works to care for and provide for the sick, poor and outcast people in areas all over the world.

Her totally devoted life of service has not gone without notice. She has received the Pope John XXIII Peace Prize (1971), the John F. Kennedy International Award (1971), The Templeton Award for "Progress in Religion" (1975), and the Nobel Peace Prize (1979). And the awards and tributes of respect continue. But the greatest award pos-

sible for her is new life breathed back into the body of one of her homeless or outcast friends, stricken with poverty, illness or hunger. Sister Teresa, not so quietly, goes about doing her work! Her life reminds all of us of the power and potential of a life that finds a religious foundation and spiritual meaning, enabling one to transcend the everyday pitfalls of this world. Her story is essential reading for everyone who seeks to develop a stronger sense of life's meaning and purpose.

How do you go about changing? How can you be different? After all, you have spent your life-time, to this point, learning how to be the way you are! If your scores are lower, however, your way of "being" thus far hasn't brought you the level of contentment you are seeking. So now is the time to consider another way.

Strategies for Change

1. Make a decision to thrive, not merely survive.

This is crucial! You deserve to live! You have been given a life that belongs only to you and that only you can fully develop. Your biggest hurdle is believing that you can be more than you are; that you can have more than you have; that you are important, rather than unimportant! It's an attitude adjustment and you must deal with it as such. There is an old proverb that says, "You can ACT your way into a new feeling quicker than you can FEEL your way into a new action!" Start! Make a beginning, the rest will follow.

2. Identify what it is that you have not yet done in life that is important to you.

Make a list if necessary! One of the reasons your life is not as enriching to you, or satisfying, is because you have some disappointments that linger. There are things you have not done that you wanted to do in life, and you have given up planning for them! Don't do it! That's what happens when death replaces life in us. But remember, you're able to read this book now because you have "life" in you! So get at those things that are still beckoning you.

3. Write an epitaph you would be comfortable having others write on your tombstone.

Now, before you write this off as a totally off-the-wall idea, remember we all have some idea of the kind of legacy we would like to leave others, and some idea of the way we would like to be remembered. Put yours into the form of a brief epitaph. Doing this will help to motivate you toward the pursuit or fulfillment of tasks necessary in bringing this focus into reality. Rod Deighan, President and CEO of Patrick-Douglas, a very successful out-placement firm in Cleveland, Ohio, calls this legacy "your thumbprint." What kind of thumbprint do you wish to leave in this world?

4. Plan the rest of your life.

This is not a plea for a day by day schedule of events, but a suggestion that you instead make a list of events to see or participate in and a list of people who are important to you and with whom you intend and want to spend time. When people make this kind of list, they often find it helpful to engage in rethinking life events, or doing what the noted gerontologist Robert Butler calls a "life review." If you are a person who tends to do this, a word of caution: Do this life review with someone whose presence will keep you from getting bogged down, seeing only your failings and shortcomings in life. Just having someone with you keeps you in touch with the successes and virtues of your life, as well. Also, realize that planning your life can mean several things! It can mean planning certain events, activities, or goals. It can also mean planning a certain approach to living. Deciding to place a strong emphasis on pleasures of the moment and living robustly in the here and now, is a plan! Helping the present and the future to become important to us is an enhancement to one's life meaning.

We have learned a great deal about life changes, retirement and other phases of our life cycle. One of the most important things we have learned is that there isn't "one way" or even a "right way" to approach this stage of life. Instead, what we have discovered is that each person has "his/her way"! Being as content, in control, and at peace with "our way" as we possibly can provides us with the foundation we need for a high level of life meaning.

Suggested Resources

Anson, Ofra, Antonovsky, Aaron, and Sagy, Shira, "Religiosity and Well-Being Among Retirees: A Question of Causality," *Behavior, Health and Aging*, Summer-Fall 1990, Vol. 1, No. 2, p. 85.

Fletcher, Wesla L. and Hansson, Robert O., "Assessing the Social Components of Retirement Anxiety," *Psychology and Aging*, March 1991, Vol. 6, No. 1, p. 76.

Frankl, V.E., *Man's Search For Meaning; An Introduction to Logotherapy*. New York: Washington Square Press, 1963.

Frankl, Viktor, "Facing the Transitoriness of Human Existence," *Generations*, Fall 1990, Vol. 14, No. 4, p. 7.

Gould, Roger, *Transformations*. New York: Simon & Schuster, 1978.

Kubler-Ross, E., *On Death and Dying*. New York: Macmillan, 1969.

Levinson, Daniel J., *The Seasons of a Man's Life*. New York: Knopf, 1978.

Richardson, Virginia, "Adjustment to Retirement: Continuity vs. Discontinuity," *International Journal of Aging and Human Development*, 1991, Vol. 33, No. 2, p. 151.

Seeber, James J., "Ministry with Retired Professionals," *Journal of Religious Gerontology*, 1990, Vol. 7, No. 1–2, p. 185.

Wingrove, C. Ray, and Slevin, Kathleen F., "Sample of Professional and Managerial Women: Success in Work and Retirement," *Journal of Women and Aging*, 1991, Vol. 3, No. 2, p. 95.

Audio-Visual Resources

Rohn, Jim, *The Art of Exceptional Living*. Nightingale-Conant Corp., PO Box 845, Morton Grove, IL 60053-9921 (PH 1 (800) 525-9000).

❖ Chapter Nine ❖
Leisure Interests

Definition: *The degree to which you expend personal energy in non-work pursuits, the objective of which is to rest your body or stimulate your mind, and the purpose of which is to find expanded meaning in your life.*

James Moreland, III

"Jim" Moreland is the Senior Vice President of Moreland Tractor Company. He is 41 years old and destined to become, in only two years, the President and CEO. His current responsibilities center around the production area of the company. He is responsible for some 725 people in this one division. His grandfather had started the company and Jim will be the third "Moreland" to serve as President and CEO. The name "Moreland" is known throughout the area, and Jim is very proud to be the next in line to run this fine company.

And Jim is ready! Or, he will be after this three year stint as production supervisor is finished. This is the final piece in his self-designed plan to prepare himself to run the company. His father, currently President and CEO, had wanted Jim to take over several years ago. Jim had resisted the move then because he wanted to be sure, in his own mind, that he was ready. Since then,he has been going about his own preparation very methodically.

Actually, this is Jim's typical style in approaching any new responsibility. Jim did not do anything that he did not do well. Rarely was he on the losing end of anything he participated in. Maybe being James R. Moreland, III, had something to do with that philosophy. He has always felt considerable pressure to succeed. He is quite athletic, and while in school these competitive needs found frequent and ready outlets in high school sports. After college, it has been a bit more difficult to find time for his interest in sports participation.

Consequently, Jim had plunged into his work at the plant. He had a lot to learn and he'd gone about learning it with a vengeance. After all, his father was the CEO and his grandfather had been the CEO. He was going to show people he was the heir apparent because he deserved it, not just because he was a Moreland. He worked long hours, he studied after hours, he did his work better than most others and spent enormous energy building a reputation that said he deserved to be the CEO on his merit, not because he was part of the Moreland family.

People worry about him because he works so hard. His wife worries about him because he isn't home much and he is so intense when he is home. Jim says, "Don't worry about me! I've learned how to relax and get away from work too!" What Jim means is that he plays racquetball at noon three times a week, jogs four miles a day the other four days, and plays 18 holes of golf at least weekly. And he plays to win! On those rare occasions when he doesn't win, his family doesn't even like to see him come home! Jim plays the way he works! Hard, fast and intensely!

Recently, however, really only within the past several months, something has changed. Something in Jim's "internal world" seems to be different. He has begun to notice that when he comes home from work he often seems tired. He is also beginning to take note of the fact that when he comes home from his leisure pursuits, he is also tired. Somehow they don't seem to be providing the fun they had always before produced in his life. He is really beginning to wonder if he is on the right track in terms of the way he approaches his life and particularly his need for relaxation. On more than one occasion he has even asked himself if he is beginning to burn out? Has he been doing something wrong?

As a matter of fact, he has! Jim has been making the mistake many energetic, hard-driving people make. He is simply transferring the same competitiveness he felt in the work place to the racquetball court, or the tennis court, or the golf course, or the weight room at the local gym. Man people "work" as intensely and rigorously to find relaxation in leisure time pursuits as they do to achieve excellence at their jobs. In most cases, this approach to leisure and relaxation is better than not doing anything. But it doesn't fit in with the definitions of leisure time activities now beginning to find expression in the experiences of thousands of retirees across our land who face the issue directly every day of their lives. Too many people are finding that their work and their leisure are similar: competitive, intense, and serious.

Relationship to Retirement

Bruce Morehouse, Ph.D., is a practicing leisure consultant in Santa Monica, California. He has a business that he calls The Leisure Company. He counsels people on what to do in their spare time. He believes most people select a leisure time activity based on what their friends are doing or what seems to be popular at the time. They really don't know, or have never discovered what it is that allows them to have fun. He asks clients to fill out a questionnaire that is designed to help them understand what really motivates them towards leisure time activities, and what they really are seeking in terms of rewards or pay-offs. Morehouse says the reasons people are motivated toward leisure time are found in the general categories of mental stimulation, social stimulation, physical competency, risk-taking, and a need for solitude. These are the basic needs they are trying to meet as they use their leisure moments. His theory is that once you understand what you're really looking for, you can select an activity that is appropriate to your need! (And all this time you've been thinking all you had to do was go out and play a little golf!—Isn't that right?)

Leisure, or play, is anything you elect to do when you're not being forced or asked to do something else. Some people say their work is their leisure. For most of us, work is too structured and too demanding to really qualify as leisure. Real leisure activities, however, must be more fluid, flexible, able to just happen, and certainly more under our own direction to fully qualify as leisure activities.

There also is a lot of confusion about what can legitimately be defined as a leisure activity. People are now finding out that real success in the realm of leisure time activity does not depend solely upon the activity chosen. The really critical factor is whether or not you are doing it by choice and you are in control of the activity. For example, if you are a salesman and play golf with a customer to strengthen your business relationship and add to future sales, golf is not a leisure time activity. In the same vein, even the simple act of watching television can become suspect.

You've been working hard writing up the annual report for your home office all day. You come home exhausted, plop down in front of the TV and growl at anyone who even attempts to talk to you for the first hour. You look and act like the typical "couch potato" as you stare with glazed eyes at whatever happens to be on TV. Is this a leisure time activity? Hardly! Psychologists would call this a "total compensatory reaction to an energy-depleted state resulting from too much work at the office"! You're vegetating! You could be doing almost anything and you wouldn't care at that point. Of course, it does serve some kind of recuperative purpose for you; eventually you're able to get up and start moving around again. We are simply making the point that you dare not confuse this "activity" with real leisure time: the objective of which is to *really rest your body and stimulate your mind, the purpose of which is to expand the meaning in your life*.

Retirement is often viewed as a time of leisure. In fact, the traditional conception of retirement is built around the belief that it *is* a time of leisure. We ran into a very young 63 year old retiree a short time ago. During the course of our conversation, the subject of volunteer workers for a community project came up. Without thinking, one of us asked, "Why don't you organize some of your retired friends? You've all got time!" He looked at us like we had absolutely lost our senses! And we thought to ourselves, "You've done it again!" Later, we realized we'd unintentionally hit upon a common bias and insensitivity toward retired people.

Far too many of us have been programmed to view retirement as time when people wander aimlessly, without purpose, looking for ways to pass time. Well, that concept is changing! And so is our understanding of the important role leisure time has to play in our retirement years. For more and more retired persons, retirement is becoming a very focused, opportunity-filled time of life, geared to the pursuit of activities, self-growth and personal sharing. People want to establish a legacy of hope, courage, inspiration and peace that will last in this world's memory long after they have gone on!

What is becoming very clear to us is the fact that those persons entering into retirement who have demonstrated at least one well-defined leisure interest achieve higher levels of success than those without leisure interests. A successful leisure interest keeps people alive, feeling creative and optimistic. It also brings real relaxation to the body and allows it to heal and rejuvenate itself with power and wholeness. The presence or absence of a leisure pursuit is an important predictor of success in retirement.

Higher scores on your RSP on this factor would indicate that you have developed your leisure interests to the point they've become satisfying priorities in your life. You do things that give you stimulation and bring rest and relaxation to your body. You have "found" or "have been found by" some of the right activities for you!

If your scores are low, it's an indication that you are probably a person who considers your "work" to be serving the purpose of leisure/fun/and relaxation. This belief will also serve to motivate you to avoid retirement. Retirement will not appear attractive to you because it will seem like such a major adjustment and change to your lifestyle. Thinking about a change of this magnitude will feel a bit monumental and for most people will cause considerable anxiety. Whenever one views retirement as "life after work," it implies a major change and a giant step into the unknown. Is it any wonder people with scores in this lower range choose to somehow avoid retirement? Avoiding it only makes sense! Being aware of this issue in your life is, of course, the first step toward being able to consider changes that will be easier to accomplish.

Projection for Success in Retirement

Persons scoring high on Factor 9 generally anticipate a higher level of activity in retirement than those who score low. High scorers can be expected to retire earlier rather than later and will usually remain permanently out of the labor market. They will not be particularly interested in becoming a "retread" (one who re-enters the labor market after retiring once). Generally, the higher your demonstrated leisure interest before retirement, the more satisfying and successful your retirement will be for you.

Those who score high in the Expectations (E-scale) but relatively low on the Present Behaviors (PB-scale) recognize the need for leisure and want to plan for it. However, because they have not yet exercised their plan in any concrete way, they have not genuinely committed themselves to the cultivation of leisure pursuits.

As we stated above, if you have lower scores on both scales, you will probably retreat from retirement because you are somewhat fearful of constructing an entirely new lifestyle. If you do retire, you are likely to become a "retread," usually finding traditional retirement nonstimulating and unfulfilling. Other retirement success factors which influence the leisure factor and which can together help you develop a broader spectrum of comparison are:

- Factor 2 – Attitude Toward Retirement
- Factor 4 – Health Perceptions
- Factor 6 – Current Life Satisfaction
- Factor 13 – Familial and Marital Issues
- Factor 15 – Replacement of Work Functions

What can you do to make changes?

Strategies for Change

No one can dispute the fact that everyone who finds themselves with time on their hands finds something to do with it. However, as we become more sophisticated and experienced in life planning, the positive and healthful benefits from leisure time usage take on greater significance. "Killing time," "using time," "filling time" become less attractive options to us. We want to live! Therefore, it becomes increasingly important for us to know what we want from leisure time activities. Do we want them to help us learn and be more creative? Are we looking for greater social interaction through our leisure activities? Do we strive for some area to compete in, to measure our development or insights against others? Are we in need of activities that we can do alone? Have we found suitable ingredients that take care of our needs for adventure and excitement? Real leisure activities meet our most important needs in these areas.

1. Make a decision to experiment with some different areas of activity.

The only thing that is certain by your not making this decision is that your life will not change! You've already learned that you need some changes in your current lifestyle.

2. Enroll in some adult education classes.

Try out some areas that are new to you but in which you may have an interest. A side advantage will be meeting other people who are growing and looking for new ideas and adventures as well. School, classes and education can be exciting when you're going purely to meet some of your own personal goals.

3. Plan one new leisure time activity per month for the next six months that would provide a new experience for you.

Don't make any immediate decisions about this activity; just let yourself experience it. Make a decision about its real interest to you several months later—on the basis of whether or not you find yourself wanting to do it again.

4. Be willing to change.

Look upon this as a time in your life when you have permission to try new things and make your own decisions about whether or not they are fun, satisfying, enriching to you and worth making a permanent part of your life. Some you will never want to do again; don't! Some you will want to do once in a while; great! Some you may want to do on a regular basis! What an important discovery!

5. Get more information.

One place to begin is by writing to "The Leisure Company," 2730 Wilshire Boulevard, Suite 350, Santa Monica, CA 90403; or call (213) 829-7430. For a price, they will have you fill out a profile and then give you information tailored to your leisure needs. Dr. Bruce Morehouse, Director, says "If stress in the workplace, stress with the children, never having enough time for fun, never meeting new people, or a host of other complaints affect your ability to have a good time, then The Leisure Company may have just the right program for you."

6. Develop a ministry of helping.

Psychologists now agree that "altruism" does exist, and, furthermore, helping others is one of the most wellness enhancing activities you can do. Helping others in need rejuvenates the soul, brings warmth to the heart, and generally stimulates the forces of wellness that produce your sense of positive well-being.

Leisure time can bring a broad smile to your face! It's your time! Your very own special time to do with as you please. If you take the time and permit yourself to try some new experiences, you will find activities that refresh your body's physical energy and your mind's creative spirit! You will be successful!

Suggested Resources

Basini, A., "Education for Leisure: A Sociological Critique," *Work and Leisure*, Ed. by Waworth, J. T. and Smith, M. A., London: Lepus Books, 1975.

Blazey, Michael A., "Travel and Retirement Status," *Annals of Tourism Research*, 1992, Vol. 19, No. 4, p. 771.

Bolles, R. N., *The Three Boxes of Life*. Calif.: Ten Speed Press, 1978.

Corbin, H. D. and Tait, W. J., *Education for Leisure*. New Jersey: Prentice-Hall, 1973.

Csikszentmihalyi, Mihaly, *Flow: The Psychology of Optimal Experience*. New York: Harper & Row.

Epperson, A., Witt, P. A. and Hitzhusen, G. (Eds.), *Leisure Counseling*. Illinois: C. C. Thomas, 1977.

Lefkowitz, Bernard, *Leisure*. New York: Hawthorne Books, 1979.

Kelly, J. R., "Work and Leisure: A Simplified Paradigm," *Journal of Leisure Research*, 1974, *6*, 1181–1193.

Neulinger, J., *The Psychology of Leisure*. Illinois: Charles C. Thomas, 1974.

Overs, R. P., Taylor, S. and Adkinson, C., *A Vocational Counseling Manual; A Complete Guide to Leisure Counseling*, Washington, D. C.: Hawkins & Associates, 1977.

Audio-Visual Resources

Covey, Stephen R., *The Seven Habits of Highly Effective People*. Nightingale-Conant Corp., PO Box 845, Morton Grove, IL 60053-9921 (PH 1 (800) 525-9000).

❖ Chapter Ten ❖
Adaptability

Definition: *The degree of personal flexibility you exercise at any given time in any given situation.*

Being alive means you are always dealing with changes. This may not be terribly profound, but it is a very significant thought to digest and integrate into your life plan. Through observation of yourself and the normal events occurring daily in your own life, you have known this for a long time. The only thing that does not change is the fact that things do change.

Change is with us and around us every day of our lives! We even use a special vocabulary to talk about and explain "change." We talk about people changing their minds, losing interest, moving on because they're bored, out-growing relationships, no longer feeling challenged, changing jobs or careers, etc. The way we express our awareness of change about ourselves and life often fills a large part of our daily conversation with friends. Consider for just a moment this not too unusual scenario from the life of a young couple dealing with an ordinary life event.

Bill and Nancy

Bill and Nancy will be so glad to get home! It always seems to be like this when they get away from their jobs, get the kids in the car, and head for the farm. Bill and Nancy live with their three children in the city. Bill is the marketing director for an automotive parts company and Nancy works as the supervisor of computer operations in a downtown department store. They work hard and both have very demanding jobs. Evenings often find them pouring over papers and proposals not finished during their regular office hours. When they are able to get away from work, they really enjoy it.

Bill grew up on a farm about 170 miles away. His parents, now retired, still live there in the house originally built by Bill's grandfather. It always felt good to get there! Everything is so peaceful out in the country. The nicest thing about it is that everything always looks the same. The trees get a little older, and the buildings sometimes get a bit shabby if you catch them in between the fresh coats of paint that seem to be regularly applied. Basically, however, it is always the same. The air is clean, the stars are vivid and clear in the evening sky, and the crops always look good. Even inside, it is always the same. Bill's folks like the house and are content with the older style of furniture. Their needs seem to be simple and neither of them ever seem to want anything that is not already there. For Bill and Nancy, it seems like an oasis. Here is one part of their world that seems to remain constant.

Bill's folks would write the scenario a bit differently. Bill's father stopped farming seven years ago after a heart attack. He had not planned to stop, but the physician told him it was time. That heart attack had literally scared the life out of Bill's father. His world has not been the same since. Now he rents their land to a neighbor to farm, and he and Bill's mother watch from the window. Living in the country is still enjoyable, but now it gets a bit boring. They worry more because it is becoming obvious that the work of keeping the buildings up is a real problem for them. Should they move into town now, or try and stay where they are and hire the help they need? It is hard to talk to Bill or their daughter about it because they both live so far away and are always busy. Maybe they just have to hang on for awhile and see what life brings. One thing Bill's folks know for sure: things will change!

George and Louisa

George and Louisa are "snowbirds"! They have been going South for the holidays for several years and plan to move to California soon, when Louisa retires. They converted various assets into cash and purchased a home just outside of San Francisco, one of their favorite spots. They planned to rent the property until they are ready to move there permanently. Five days after they closed on the property sale, George was hit from behind at a stop sign. His injuries were fatal. For Louisa, life will never be the same again!

Ben

Ben has worked for United Lighting Corporation for 29 years! He is 53 years old and has been entrenched as the supervisor in his department for the past seven years. When he retires, in another eight years, he'll have a nice pension, his home will be paid for, and he and Sharon can take some of those trips they have been putting off. It feels good.

The change comes in the form of a terse announcement the next day at work. The company has been purchased by J S & R Electric Corporation, effective immediately. An administrative decision to cut 12 positions has been made. Ben's is one of them. He is offered the option to move to another city, some 700 miles away, and work for the company. Or he could accept a severance package worth 50% of his annual salary for the next three years. CHANGE has entered his life again!

Relationship to Retirement

Factor 10, Adaptability, relates very directly to retirement. Persons who cannot adjust to changes will find that retirement poses a difficult transition. Generally, persons who are rigid view their world through a filter that takes out everything except things they want to see. This kind of attitude does not encourage success in retirement.

How adaptable to change are you? Your degree of adaptability is determined by many factors. First, your life experiences to date provide you with an adaptability foundation. Were you an only child who always got your way, or the middle child in a brood of ten, forced to adapt at every turn in your childhood? What kind of family was yours? Was it rigid, dogmatic, authoritarian, or was it more mellow and "laid back"? In your work, are you encouraged to be flexible, or are you the keeper of the Standard Operating Procedures Manuals? What are your religious beliefs and values? Are you known as being very opinionated or do you generally "roll with the punches"? Are you more like a palm tree that sways and bends in the wind? Or, are you more like an oak tree that stands rigid against the storm, until it either survives or breaks? Although we encourage the growth of palm trees, there isn't a right or wrong answer to the above questions. All that is "right" is that you think these issues through and be aware of some of the ways they have influenced your life.

Ed

Ed is 47 years old. As of six days ago, he is also unemployed! It had happened suddenly. At least, it seemed sudden to him! Ed had been on the move in his company. He had worked his way up and through the intricacies of the corporate ladder until he was given consideration for the position of Vice President in the marketing division. Actually, he was one of two finalists for the position, the other being a man Ed had known and worked with for years in the same department. He is also a man Ed has never been able to get along with. They always seem to be on the opposite sides of issues and decisions. Ed can not tolerate it. It is always obvious to him that Jack just does not understand all the implications of his proposals. In fact, if Ed is questioned, he will even admit openly that he does not consider Jack to be very bright. He has never said that directly to Jack, but he has hinted at it.

Ed is not one to be intimidated or pushed around. He also is not interested in a lot of new ideas or changes in policy! Jack, on the other hand, seems to always be pushing for new ways of doing things and devising different strategies to market the same product. Ed knows the old ideas are best! Why can't others see it?

Maybe because they see something else. When Jack was given the job as Vice President, Ed was told his job was over. The reason, they said was an attitude that could not see change and incorporate new ideas into a modern marketing philosophy. Ed left the company with his attitude intact and unchanged! Not surprisingly, it has re-

mained intact. However, even as it has not helped him in his work, neither will he find it helpful nor encouraging to his success in retirement.

Retirement requires life-style and self-definition changes of a monumental degree. Not only are you forced to change your daily routine, but you no longer have your work to remind you of who you are. Retirement forces you to think of yourself in very different terms. All this requires great flexibility and great personal adjustment, both of which are central traits of adaptability.

Some scientists claim it is our human ability to adapt that has allowed us to thrive to the degree we have. Quite likely this is true. Certainly we know that if a person cannot adapt to a situation with some degree of ease, they will either leave or die. Other persons will expend so much energy trying to adapt that they simply get sick. Successful retirement requires great amounts of acceptance, forgiveness and an attitude of tolerance, as well as a positive disposition toward other people—better known as "accommodation."

In 1983, Morton Lieberman and Sheldon Tobin, two noted social scientists, published a book called *The Experience of Old Age*. In this book they published findings gleaned from their study of stress generated in the lives of over 600 elderly people who found it necessary for various reasons to relocate. They focused their studies on four conditions that contribute to one's adaptive capacities to help them through such an obvious time of stress. Those four conditions they studied were:

1. physical capacity.
2. mental capacity.
3. energy potential.
4. social resources.

The authors concluded that maintaining a strong sense of self and identity is the central and most crucial task facing all elderly, whether they face relocation or normal life adjustments.

Projection for Success in Retirement

How adaptable do you see yourself? The E and PB scores you achieved give you a unique insight into your personal adaptability. They combine your sense of what you need to retire successfully with your perspective of current behavioral maturity.

What do your scores mean? If your PB score is higher, it indicates a high level of retirement readiness in your ability to adapt; and you are to be congratulated! You have already learned the values of being flexible and have been able to avoid numerous difficulties in adjusting to life experiences. You incorporate change as a part of your life without it throwing you off course or escalating into a major crisis. Your strong inner sense of self remains solid and steers you through changes without allowing you to be de-railed.

If you have a PB score identifying your adaptability as being low, you may not find it easy to adjust to the changes and transitions retirement requires. You may even feel that you cannot, or will not adjust to change. Having this attitude leaves you vulnerable to an emotional and defensive response to the changes you do confront. Family and close friends usually do not find that quality easy to tolerate. It will also build increasingly toward higher levels of stress as you are confronted with further life changes. You will want to investigate ways to increase your level of tolerance and flexibility.

Other factors in your Profile have a direct influence on your ability to tolerate change and unexpected events. These factors include:

- Factor 1 – Work Disengagement
- Factor 3 – Directedness
- Factor 4 – Health Perceptions
- Factor 11 – Identity With Past Stages
- Factor 14 – Replacement of Work Functions

If any of your behavioral scores are in the lower or even mid-range areas on these factors, there will be some corresponding influence on your scores in Factor 10. Finding better ways to balance one area of your life usually affects other areas in positive ways.

Sarah

Consider for a moment the transition facing Sarah. Sarah is 57 years old and has been widowed for the past 22 years. During this time she has finished raising three children and worked steadily as the office manager and bookkeeper in a small office supply company, a position she has held for the past 26 years. Sarah was raised as an only child in her original family, even though she actually had a brother. Her brother was born to her parents late in their lives and is mentally retarded. Sarah's parents raised him and kept him with them throughout his life. They were farm people and lived in the same place all of Sarah's life. Her father died 15 years ago and her mother is now in the intensive care unit of their local hospital where she is fighting cancer. Her prognosis is poor. Her one request of Sarah is that she provide for and support her mentally retarded brother. He is now 44 years old but totally dependent upon his mother and the support Sarah has been able to give these past few years. Sarah's plan is to quit her job, move into her parents' home and take over their role with her brother when her mother dies. Her question to us was, can she do it?

Sarah is not an adaptable person. Nothing in her life has ever prepared her to handle such a responsibility and she really does not want to do it. When her husband died suddenly, her parents had stepped in to offer guidance, direction and support, as she put together a new plan. Now her children have married and moved from the community, so her life revolves around her job, which has remained the same for the past years. Her Retirement Success Profile indicates that Sarah is heavily involved and identifies with her work; her directedness score shows that she feels she has little control over her life; her life meaning scale is low; she is heavily invested emotionally in events in her past; and her age perception score shows her to be a person who feels very young. She has energy and a desire to do things that have never gotten done! Sarah is not ready to make the kind of transition she's considering. (Through conversations, we are able to make other arrangements for her brother and suggestions for her own life that open doors to the future for her.)

Paul

In contrast to Sarah, consider the transition Paul faces. Paul is 64 years old and plans to retire in two months. A friend asked him if he is ready for such a change and he said he had not really thought about it, but would. He asked us to help him decide if he is ready!

Paul is an engineer. He is the fourth child in a family of six children. His father had a variety of jobs during his working life and had taken the family with him to most parts of the country. Paul remembers, for example, being in four different schools during one term. He served as a pilot in the army during World War II and then came home to finish his engineering degree. His first job was with an oil firm that sent him around the world checking out rumors of oil. This was followed by several supervisory positions. During this period of his life, he managed to get married and raise four children of his own from two marriages. Further, Paul has a retirement plan. He wants to build a solar energy A-frame cabin on a piece of land he owns in Colorado. Paul is ready to retire. His Adaptability score is quite high, his Attitude Toward Retirement is very positive and he feels quite secure with his financial planning. In addition, he is in good health and feels youthful—maintaining a high energy level that points him toward a very active retirement lifestyle. Paul's plan is on target for his level of retirement preparation.

Strategies for Change

If you want to become more flexible, what can you do?

1. Start by taking a look at yourself.

How do you think others see you? As a risk taker? Adventuresome? Perhaps even a bit unpredictable? Think about your own image of yourself as a person. That is where you begin. Can you see yourself stepping outside the lines you have so carefully drawn for yourself throughout these years? Can you imagine yourself doing things you have not done before? Living in a style that you may only have dreamed about? Saying things, doing things, being someone you have only dreamed of before?

When starting school, we are taught to color only between the lines in our coloring book. We are praised for being careful, good, and for following instructions. How many five year old children will resist that kind of influence? The result is that we get hooked and often develop patterns of behavior that can take the better part of our lives to understand and change. In most of us, there are segments of our personalities that have never been permitted free expression. Can you express your life outside your traditional boundaries? This will be important to you as you seek to increase your adaptability scores.

2. Start with an area of your life over which you have control.

Change some of your personal habits that can be changed easily, just to capture a sense of what it is like to do things differently. You could, for example:

a. sit in a different chair at the table.
b. buy an article of clothing that is not practical, but it is inviting.
c. try a new exercise that might be different for you, like a brisk walk in the morning or evening; or,
d. pick up a book in a subject area you normally would not read in.

3. Take time out to reflect thoroughly on your family origin.

Taking the time we need to know our parents, brothers and sisters, grandparents, etc., can be invaluable to us in understanding our own personality patterns and habits. We all started out in families of some form and shape. Those early years had great influence in molding and establishing patterns in our lives. A thorough investigation of these influences can bring a great sense of freedom.

4. Begin where you can.

Change some of the unimportant things in your life first and get a feel for being different. Remember that making small changes or modifications in your lifestyle now could prevent you from having to make larger, more stressful changes later.

Adaptability is part of the foundation every person needs in order to move toward maturity and retirement success. Cultivating and balancing this capability in your life is well worth the effort or risk required.

Suggested Resources

Ballard, Jack and Ballard, Phoebe, *Beating the Age Game: Redefining Retirement.* New York, NY: Master Media, 1993.

Betancourt, Raoul Louis, *Retirement and Men's Physical Health.* New York, NY: Garland Pub., 1991.

Brady, E. Michael, *Retirement. The Challenge of Change.* Univ. of Southern Maine, 1988.

Bridges, William, *Transitions.* New York: Addison-Wesley, 1980.

Ekerdt, David J., "Marital Complaints in Husband-Working and Husband-Retired Couples," *Research on Aging*, Sept. 1991, Vol. 13, No. 3, p. 364.

Gibson, Rose, "Subjective Retirement of Black Americans," *Journals of Gerontology*, July 1991, Vol. 46, No. 4, p. S204.

Neugarten, B. L., *Adult Personality: Toward a Psychology of the Life Cycle.* Chicago: University of Chicago Press, 1968.

Neugarten, B. L., *Middle Age and Aging.* Chicago: University of Chicago Press, 1968.

Reeves, Joy B., and Darville, Ray L., "Aging Couples in Dual-Career/Earner Families: Patterns of Role-Sharing," *Journal of Women and Aging*, 1992, Vol. 4, No. 1, p. 39.

Reis, Myrna and Gold, Dolores P., "Retirement, Personality and Life Satisfaction: A Review and Two Models," *Journal of Applied Gerontology*, June 1993, Vol. 12, No. 2, p. 261.

Richardson, Virginia E., *Retirement Counseling: A Handbook for Gerontology Practitioners*. New York, NY: Springer Pub., 1993.

Szinovacz, Maximiliane, and Washo, Christine, "Gender Differences in Exposure to Life Events and Adaptation to Retirement," *Journals of Gerontology*, July 1992, Vol. 47, No. 4, p. S191.

Vaillant, George E., *Adaptation to Life*. Boston: Little, Brown & Co., 1977.

Vinick, Barbara H., and Ekerdt, David J., "Retirement: What Happens to Husband-Wife Relationships?," *Journal of Geriatric Psychiatry*, 1991, Vol. 24, No. 1, p. 23.

Toffler, Alvin, *The Adaptive Corporation*. New York: McGraw Hill, 1985.

Audio-Visual Resources

Silva, Laura, *The Silva Method in Action*. Nightingale-Conant Corp., PO Box 845, Morton Grove, IL 60053-9921 (PH 1 (800) 525-9000).

❖ Chapter Eleven ❖
Identification with Past Life Stages

Definition: *The degree to which you live in the present and find your current life fulfilling, rather than "living in the past."*

Ned

Ned's knees are actually wobbly! He can't believe he is doing this. He had already been to the bank and gotten all the financial papers signed. Luckily, Paul, his close friend as well as his banker, hadn't asked too many questions. Ned was still too shaky to talk about this with his good friends yet. But, being a bit shaky in the knees wasn't going to stop him from doing it. No sir! Ever since he had stopped at Louie's Auto Emporium and looked at that convertible, he'd known he was going to do it. That car is going to be his! He has the money in his pocket and the car is just waiting for him now. In two hours or less, he'd be driving out of the car lot and down Belview Drive! He will have the top down, and he'll drive slowly enough so he can watch people look at him as he drives by. Because they are going to look! This car is so sleek, has such clean lines and gives that look of polished sophistication! Ned is sure that he'll be noticed! In just a few hours Ned will recapture a piece of his youth!

Nancy

Nancy is so excited! Finally she is going to get some action. It had taken a long time, but it would be worth it. At first, the doctor hadn't wanted to do the surgery. He had suggested diets, vitamins, exercise and several other alternatives. There is some risk, evidently, but it didn't seem too great to Nancy. Living without the surgery also seemed very unpleasant to Nancy. For five years she had been thinking about doing this. Within this past year, it had really become important, however. Her skin seemed to be drooping and sagging more in the past weeks. Maybe she's just so aware of it now that she is waiting for her day in surgery.

Dr. Fellon came highly recommended. She had talked to a friend of Mary's who'd had this same surgery and was very happy with the results. Mary's friend said she thought she looked fifteen years younger now than she did before she'd had the face lift surgery. Nancy could hardly wait! Getting old was a terribly embarrassing experience. She had always prided herself on her youthful appearance and good looks. In high school and college she'd always been quite attractive, even striking, in her appearance. People had always told her how beautiful she was. She had so enjoyed those comments and they had meant so much to her. She'd felt special and, yes, even beautiful!

But she hasn't felt that way for the past five years at least. Her skin doesn't have that nice tone to it that she had once taken such pride in. Her face lift will cure that. She's certain of it! She was a little uneasy about what Dr. Fellon had said when he talked about the slight possibility of nerve damage. But, she guessed, that was something he had to always say to patients, because she knew in surgery of this type that possibility always existed. But the chances are quite remote. Her friends reassured her of that. She will be beautiful again! She will feel like her old self and she will have friends again! She should have had this done earlier. Tomorrow her life will be like she wanted it again; just as it once had been.

Ned and Sally are emotionally pulled to previous stages of life development. Their attempts to change their lives are efforts to recapture a time in their lives when they had found living more exciting and fun than they do now. They both fear losing something of value.

Ned had some needs thwarted at an earlier time in his life when he wasn't able to do anything about it. When he was 22 years old, he really wanted a new convertible. He wanted it more than anything else in the world at that time. But he'd just graduated from college and had no job of his own. His wife was working part time and together they were trying to raise a two-year old daughter. It was hardly the time to satisfy a boyhood dream. Ned told himself then that someday he would have that car! The car represented many things to him when he was 22. It symbolized freedom, power and an element of control in his life that he hadn't possessed then. Ned put that yearning—that emotional need—on-the-shelf for these last 24 years. Now, he's going to take that need off the shelf, dust it off, and put it to rest once and for all by getting that convertible. In the process, he's going to feel just like he would have felt when he was 22 years old, 24 years ago. Or so he thinks.

Nancy struggles with issues from her past, too. Her struggle centers around an internal picture she carries in her mind of a beautiful, attractive young woman, popular and in-demand. Nancy's self-esteem and ego-needs are all tied up with the way she looks and relate only marginally to the person she knows herself to be on the inside. In fact, she is totally convinced that if others knew her the way she knows herself, she would have no friends. She feels shallow and confused about who she is. Sometimes she doesn't even feel worthwhile as a person!

Regaining a youthful appearance became increasingly important to Nancy as she got older. Preserving her appearance, recapturing her looks, is her way of regaining a time in her life when she felt important, sought after, and looked up to. Her surgery will bring that time back to her! Or so she thinks.

What do *you* think? Do Ned and Nancy remind you of anyone you know? Well, there are a lot of Neds and Nancy's around us. That's one of the reasons why this factor eleven, Identification with Past Life Stages, is so important in your retirement success.

Looking to the Past

Everyone can look back and find times in their past when they were particularly successful, happy, productive, fulfilled, and felt physically attractive. What factor eleven suggests, however, is that not only do some people believe their past life phases may have been better, they even want somehow to go back to those times in a deliberate effort to avoid the current life stage they are in. This factor suggests that one can actually feel a reluctance to become fully involved in life around them because they believe it could never "live-up" to the success of some previous life stage. This belief translates quickly into the conviction that this current life stage has little or nothing to offer. People "live through it," or unconsciously pass through it without ever allowing themselves to taste it, smell it, feel it or think rationally about what this phase of life has to offer them.

Picture, if you will, a person wearing surgical garb: footlets, plastic gloves, a face mask, paper hat and coveralls. They can't physically touch or be touched. Nothing of themselves is exposed! They are sterile! This is a bit like some people who allow themselves to live through certain phases of their lives when they can't emotionally connect. They can retreat back into a memory of when things were what they needed them to be. Life was safe, satisfying or whatever it took to make that particular time in their lives so memorable. By fastening onto this past life stage, they can lock-out any intrusion from the present life stage. Nothing that happens can ever be as good! No experience can ever be as exciting! No real life event can ever have the potential or hope of being the best time of their life!

Emotionally difficult times from our past have the same effect. In fact, it is easier for most people to get emotionally fixated by hurtful times from their past than by the good times. A personal defeat in life, the tragic death of a loved one or family member, a prolonged illness or crippling disease, the loss of status through life events—all have the potential to emotionally block us from further personal development. If this happens, we risk locking ourselves away from the really rewarding and satisfying moments of this current life stage: unable to release ourselves from our emotional attachments of the past.

Relationship to Retirement

How does factor eleven, Identification with Past Life Stages, relate to retirement success? The relationship is a direct one. If you harbor the feeling that a particular stage in your past life was better, and consequently discount your present life, growing into the maturity required for successful retirement will be difficult for you to achieve. In fact, you probably will feel a strong pull to reach back to relive the past in the same way you did "back then." Such an attitude would certainly hinder any changes that might be necessary for you, preventing you from moving on into a personally productive and successful retirement.

Successful retirement requires that you be able to stretch and reach for new experiences. This demands an intellectual and emotional openness to your current personal development. It requires a sense of what Dr. Wayne Dyer calls "no-limit" thinking in his book *Pulling Your Own Strings*. Such thinking seeks new experiences and is continuously inviting change into your world rather than encouraging your "living in the past."

Consider for a moment an analogy drawn between Ned's life and that of a tugboat on the great Mississippi River. Tugboats push things, sometimes even pull barges up and down the river. Ned had wanted that car since he had been 22 years old. He had pulled and pushed that desire through a lot of years, using up a lot of energy. Just for a moment, think of those tugboats pulling empty barges up the Mississippi River. Our lives are not completely unlike those hard-working tugboats. We're always pulling our lives along behind us, knowing that if we want to get anywhere, we have to move upstream.

Often misfortune occurs along the way. We get loaded up with feelings of hurt, pain, humiliation, shame and guilt. But we have to keep going. So, we just throw these feelings over our shoulders into the barges we're pulling behind us and keep going. Once in a while, something very nice happens to us. But we don't have the time to enjoy it too long because we're so busy! So, over the shoulder again, into the barge. In this exact way, many,many significant moments made up of great emotional traumas get carried along in those barges we're pulling. Sometimes those barges get so heavy we can't make much headway upstream! It takes a lot of energy to pull our barges through the water and against the current! Sometimes we do well just to maintain the status quo of our progress. In fact, it often takes all our energy just to prevent ourselves from being pulled back downstream! If the barges get too heavy, they rob us of all options and potential fun along the way. Without extra energy, we can't take the time to swing over to the shore and refuel, enjoy the peacefulness of that hidden cove, or just lay anchor and enjoy ourselves. We have to keep the tension on those ropes holding the barges close to us or risk disaster.

Some people are walking around with bowed backs from pulling a lot of weight. Some people have lost all enthusiasm, zest and interest for life in general. All they can remember to do is keep the bow headed upstream and the engines running full throttle. Once in a while they shout to someone on shore for help. Sometimes they can hear the answer shouted back across the stormy river: "Cut the rope!" Those watching from along the banks of the river can see the problem. They know the answer! They feel its worth taking the risk and the loss of the barges! People on shore can hardly wait to see the surge of energy and the dramatic increase in speed the tug experiences as the barges are cut loose, one by one.

Sometimes, all one can do is to cut the rope and let the barges carrying all those emotional traumas float free. Often it's a great relief to realize that we don't have to pull everything that has happened to us in the past around with us forever.

If you are a person who worries, ruminates and/or dwells on past injuries or high points in your life, this factor may speak to you. It takes energy to live the life of a tugboat, pulling around all the emotional traumas of previous life experiences. If you spend your energy living in the past, you won't have energy available to spend in the present. Living in the present offers far greater potential for happiness, real enjoyment and certainly for genuine retirement success.

Your RSP

If your Present Behaviors score (PB-scale) on this factor is quite high, you have achieved a significant level of retirement readiness in this area of your life. Specifically, this means you exhibit a high degree of "present living," spending minimal time and energy re-living moments from the past. It means you anticipate, even expect, positive change to occur in your life and look forward to it! Your life, in general, is relatively uninhibited by an attitude of "things were better back when." You affect others in a stimulating way because you are looking for change and progress in your thinking.

Scores on this same scale that are lower, however, suggest that you identify heavily with previous life stages. Doing this allows little emotional or psychological energy for investment in current life experiences and opportunities. Feeling this way strengthens a negative attitude about the present time and leaves you fearful and resistant of what the future may hold for you. Predictably, people with scores in this range often become a bit reactionary, which further limits their circle of friends and supportive relationships. A lower score in this area means you may want to look at ways of changing that can bring you higher levels of satisfaction and retirement success.

Projection for Success in Retirement

Exactly how does your score on this factor affect your retirement decision? Persons who score high on Factor Eleven will normally seek a healthful, happy retirement. If you are a person with high scores on this factor, you will tend to have a positive attitude about life in general and expect changes to be good. You will probably retire sooner rather than later and will most likely enjoy a positive, successful retirement.

Persons who score low on this factor tend to wish things were "back the way they were." Having this attitude will not contribute to success in retirement. Other factors from the Profile that influence Factor Eleven directly are:

- Factor 3 – Directedness
- Factor 4 – Health Perception
- Factor 7 – Projected Life Satisfaction
- Factor 8 – Life Meaning
- Factor 14 – Perception of Age

Strategies for Change

In Greek mythology there is a story about the God Sysyphus whose task in life it was to push a particular rock up a hill. It was a big rock, and very heavy. Every time he seemed almost to have it to the top of the hill, it would get away from him and chase him wildly down the hill as he struggled to keep it from running over him and crushing him. When it finally rolled to a stop, he would begin his task all over again. But he never got to the top with the rock! And, nothing in the story ever changed.

Some people live their lives this way. They have many emotional scars and pitfalls from previous life experiences that have never really been settled. These experiences can become fierce obstacles, similar to that rock that Sysyphus kept trying to roll up the hill. Some folks have to run awfully fast to keep out of the way, fearful that those feelings could break loose and get out of control. Fear keeps these people locked into certain life stages and frozen into previous emotional positions they have faced in life. Until a person can deal with those feelings more realistically, either setting them or cutting them free, these stored feelings will continue to be problematic.

1. Try to identify what it is that is missing right now in your life that you need in order to be happy.

These things that are missing now are part of the reason you get stuck trying to recapture moments from the past. You may be waiting for things that will never happen! Get involved in something that is happening now!

2. Develop a plan of action that leads to some changes for you.

In a very specific way (using pencil and paper), write down the changes that you want to introduce into your life over the next two to five years. If you can't put this plan together alone, find someone to help you by listening and supporting your ideas.

3. Spend whatever time is necessary grieving over the losses you have experienced in your life.

This may not sound like fun, but it could be the only way you can move on with your life. Unresolved grief is one of the major reasons people get stuck in the past. You have to say "good-by" to the losses (or moments that can't be) before you can say "hello" to the new experiences. It is from the new experiences that you will receive energy and zest for living!

4. Believe in yourself and learn to be nice to yourself.

This may be the hardest challenge. Spend enough time alone that you genuinely know what it is that gives you pleasure and satisfaction. Then be sure you structure time for those things. Live your life in such a way that you maintain a strong sense of integrity and respect for who you are as a person.

5. Think about the advice you would give someone who asked you how to get over being locked up in an emotional moment from their past.

Would the advice you give them have relevance to your own life?

Being able to be "emotionally available" to present events, people, hopes and dreams is what brings genuine happiness and vitality to most people. Developing this area of your life will help assure you of a high level of retirement success.

Suggested Resources

"Age Wave: An Interview with Ken Dychtwald," *Training and Development Journal*, Feb 1990, Vol. 44, No. 2, p. 22.

Bridges, William, *Transitions*. New York: Addison-Wesley, 1980.

Dyer, Wayne, *Pulling Your Own Strings*, 1987.

Harper, David J., "Remembered Work Importance, Satisfaction, Reminiscence and Adjustment in Retiring: A Case Study," Counseling Psychology Quarterly, 1993, Vol. 6, No. 2, p. 155.

Kopp, Sheldon, *An End To Innocence; Facing Life Without Illusions*. New York: Bantam Books, 1981.

Kopp, Sheldon, *Mirror, Mask and Shadow; The Risks and Rewards Of Self Acceptance*. New York: Bantam Books, 1982.

Miller, S., Wackman, D., Nunnally, E., and Saline, C., *Straight Talk*. New York: Signet, 1981.

Milletti, Mario A., *Voices of Experience. Fifteen Hundred Retired People Talk About Retirement*. Teacher's Insurance, 1987.

Pastan, Linda, *The Five Stages of Grief*. New York: W. W. Norton, 1982.

Paul, Robert J., and Townsend, James B., "Managing the Older Worker—Don't Just Rinse Away the Gray," *Academy of Management Executives*, Aug 1993, Vol. 7, No. 3, p. 67.

Williamson, Robert C., Rinehart, Alice Duffy, and Blank, Thomas O., *Early Retirement: Promises and Pitfalls*. New York, NY: Plenum Press, 1992.

Audio-Visual Resources

McGinnis, Alan Loy, *The Power of Optimism.* Nightingale-Conant Corp., PO Box 845, Morton Grove, IL 60053-9921 (PH 1 (800) 525-9000).

❖ Chapter Twelve ❖ Dependents

Definition: *The degree to which you feel your dependents, particularly your children or grandchildren and/or your aging parents, etc., require your active and continued support.*

Marvin and Linda

Marvin and Linda have to hurry home. They are still uneasy when they are gone too long. Even after seven months, it is hard to know just how much responsibility to assume for the grandchildren. Being grandparents from a distance is a vastly different experience from being "hands-on" grandparents. Even after this length of time they are still adjusting!

Marvin and Linda raised three children of their own, educated them, and rejoiced with them as they all married and moved on into new lives. Joanie had been the last to get married. Even though she was the middle child in their family, many of her experiences seemed to have come last. She and Peter had met and gotten married when she was 27 years old. For the next ten years, they had been very happy. Peter worked as a graphic designer and Joanie kept house and chose to raise their two small children at home. Fifteen months ago, Peter became ill. Actually, he had never been in very good health. He was heavy, he smoked, ate lots of junk foods and never exercised. He was first diagnosed with lung cancer. That diagnosis was quickly enlarged to include bone cancer, and he died within six months. Joanie and the two kids, Sharon and Mike, moved in with Marvin and Linda two months later.

At the time, that decision had seemed to make sense to everyone. Joanie needed a place she could afford as she adjusted to a new life. Marvin and Linda still had the big house and lots of room. They all thought it would work our nicely. But what a change. Sharon and Mike are eight and six years of age. They need a lot of attention and Joanie is having a difficult time grasping her new life as a single parent. Often, it seemed to Marvin, his daughter regressed back to being a child herself, forcing him and Linda to assume responsibility for three children once again. It certainly felt a lot more like being a parent again than he was prepared for. He is within a year of retirement! He does not know how long it will take for Joanie to get on her feet again. In fact, there are days when he does not know if she ever will! That worries him. He is not sure he or Linda have the stamina or desire to raise another family. Of one thing he's certain; he will not be able to retire next year. Those plans are gone!

Life is what Happens to Us While We Make Plans!

Marvin and Linda did not ask to be in the predicament they now face . . . but here it is. Sometimes life brings changes that we can only react to with the resources available to us at that given moment. It is not possible to anticipate or plan for events you do not think will ever happen. Marvin and Linda have been thinking of a retirement life for the two of them. Now they are back in the role of raising a young family and not sure how it has all happened to them. Life is unpredictable. "The best laid plans . . . . etc.!"

Most of us probably know people like Marvin and Linda, who have been forced to readjust their plans because of unexpected changes in the lives of their children. Life does not always follow a predictable path. Many people discover that as they live longer and life stages stretch out, some different patterns of family life begin to emerge. Two changes in particular are worth noting, because they both have a direct influence on retirement. First, children are requiring more time for transition from positions of dependence to independence. Educators and sociologists give us many reasons for this phenomenon. Our expanding and lengthening educational process certainly has extended adolescence or the time of dependence our youth need to become established in their life roles. It is not uncommon for adolescence to now extend to age 25 or even beyond. This is a big adjustment for many families to make.

A second major change affecting families is the ever increasing length of life now being reached by so many of our elders. Today, it is common for people to reach retirement only to find their parents reaching an age (85–95) when they need increased care and support. The "sandwich generation" becomes a very real phenomenon when you wake up and discover that your grown children are transitioning back into the family at the same time your parents are beginning to have greater needs for support. It is little wonder people feel caught between!

Obviously, all of this has a direct impact on retirement decisions. The more your dependents rely upon you for support, the more inclined you are to keep your life exactly the way it is. This is particularly true if these dependents are children (regardless of their age) who have yet to achieve a level of independence on their own. Support can take many forms, the most obvious being financial. Whenever your children depend upon your funds to sustain themselves to meet college expenses or help with personal bills they cannot pay, you feel the burdens of responsibility and increased financial pressures. There are many forces in today's society driving young people to require continued support from parents. Examples of these prolonged needs include: career transitions that require additional training and education, an extended illness, divorce, separation, or the death of a child's spouse. You could add to the list from your own experiences!

Occasionally another issue influences this factor. Some parents just cannot seem to encourage or give their children permission to achieve independence. They don't want them, literally or figuratively, to leave home. Some "super parents" have no idea what to do without children around to justify the roles they have developed for themselves. Sometimes children "must" remain at home because Mom and Dad could not make it together in the marriage without the kids as a buffer. In these marriages, children are assigned the unfair and unwanted task of becoming the glue keeping bad relationships together. Furthermore, in addition to living an unwanted role in life, these children often end up paying the ultimate price: the sacrifice of their own personal freedom and true adulthood.

These are common examples of family dynamics that keep children from growing up. Other examples might include: a personal feeling of guilt some parents feel in not having done enough for a child; a psychological gain some parents achieve by unconsciously keeping the child dependent; or perfectionistic thinking from some parents resulting in a demand that children "have it all" before they can be allowed to separate and achieve independence. This list is certainly not all inclusive, as the forces that motivate parental and child behavior are complex.

Projection for Success in Retirement

What do your scores mean? If your Present Behaviors score on this factor is higher, you are, at this time, generally feeling free of the responsibilities and constraints caused by dependent persons in your life. If you have children, quite likely you have launched them and now enjoy a parental role that does not include direct support. Under these circumstances, you will be much more inclined to retire. You will also find it possible to define your retirement according to your own desires, rather than being forced to give continued consideration as well as financial support to the needs of others.

Lower scores identify you as a person who carries a heavy feeling of responsibility for other people. It is a signal to you that you will want to give considerable attention to this area of your life before you make the decision to retire. Carrying this amount of responsibility for others could easily be a deterrent to you in your decision to retire, trapping you in your present work situation because of obligations you still feel to others.

Care-giver, helper, support person and guardian are all roles we play through various stages of life in our relationships with other people. Often these roles are necessary. Caring people do not live in isolation from the needs of people around them, especially if those people are members of their own family. Often life requires us to provide help, assistance, resources and counsel to others. Sometimes we are forced to assume a temporary burden while they re-adjust and get ready to take over their own responsibilities again. Certainly this happens with greater frequency for preretirees, especially in the areas of prolonged adolescence and aging parent responsibilities. We know that, on occasion, life requires us to provide this kind of help permanently, and we respond, difficult as it is, because it is a human need.

Luckily, however, these situations are the exceptions. Most people eventually arrive at a life stage where they take responsibility for themselves. Whenever possible, this is the natural, healthy pathway of life. Each generation should be taking care of its own needs, without contaminating or confusing the life paths of the generations that follow. As family therapists, we frequently deal with families who spend enormous amounts of time and energy sorting out conflicting family issues that have been passed along to them from previous generations. Family issues can get very blurred when they are shared between generations. If one generation does not take responsibility for and complete its life tasks, the next generation assumes the responsibility of their parents' unfulfilled life tasks, as well as their own life tasks. This scenario progresses just like the national debt! Before long, it feels overwhelming and no one feels capable of correcting it!

Children need to be raised with a goal of leaving home! That is the essence of parenting. Each generation needs to assume responsibility for itself, and not become an unnecessary burden to the next! Obviously, it can not always work this way, and when it does not, we make the best of the choices available to us. Your score on this factor will help you gain a clear picture of the level of responsibility for others you still carry. Knowing this should help you determine how necessary it is to carry this responsibility, or if there are other options available.

Strategies for Change

If you want to change your score, what can you do?

1. Join a support group.

None of us are more susceptible to psychological blind spots than when it comes to dealing with our dependent family members. It is extremely hard to see these issues rationally and objectively. Finding a group of other people talking about similar issues is one of the ways we can get ideas and objectivity on the problems we face. Some of the hardest questions we ever have to answer concern our children and our aging parents. Sometimes it takes much more support than we feel we have with our own resources. A group that understands can be helpful!

2. Read the literature available about dealing with adolescents who do not leave home, and aging parents who need understanding.

Most theory and educational information has a way of being re-active, rather than pro-active. Solutions do not seem to appear in writing until after problems have been observed and lived with for a time. Well, we have had the problems for a while and now we are getting some of the answers in print! Literature is appearing that speaks to these issues and family dilemmas. Don't overlook the library as a resource, especially journals about family issues and family living.

3. Use resources that marriage and family counselors bring to this area of life concern.

Children who cannot seem to leave home often are symptomatic of a family system that needs intervention. Adults who become martyrs in dealing with aging parents can often benefit from a family counselor's perspective. Watch for adult community education classes that focus on themes of family relationships.

4. Sometimes taking care of parents and children is realistic and necessary.

When it is, learn how to take care of yourself in the process. You have to find a place where you can receive nurturing and support if you are to continuously give these qualities to others. You must find the resources to re-energize yourself.

Suggested Resources

Brubaker, Timothy H., "Continuity and Change in Later Life Families: Grandparenthood, Couple Relationships and Family Caregiving," *Gerontological Review*, 1990, Vol. 3, No. 1, p. 24.

Cadmus, Robert R., *Caring For Your Aging Parents.* Englewood, New Jersey: Prentice Hall, 1984.

Calesanti, Toni M., "Bringing in Diversity: Toward an Inclusive Theory of Retirement," *Journal of Aging Studies*, Summer 1993, Vol. 7, No. 2, p. 133.

Dolan, Edward F., *How To Leave Home—And Make Everybody Like It.* Dodd Press, 1977.

Goldstein, Stanley, *Troubled Children/Troubled Parents: The Way Out.* New York: Athensum Press, 1979.

Halpern, Howard M., *Cutting Loose: An Adult Guide to Coming to Terms With Your Parents.* New York: Bantam Books, 1978.

Henretta, John C., O'Rand, Angela M. and Chan, Christopher G., "Joint Role Investments and Synchronization of Retirement: A Sequential Approach to Couples' Retirement Timing," *Social Forces*, June 1993, Vol. 71, No. 4, p. 981.

Johnson, Richard P., *Aging Parents: How To Understand and Help Them.* Liguori, MO: Liguori Press, 1987.

Skirboll, Esther and Silverman, Myrna, "Women's Retirement: A Case Study Approach," *Journal of Women and Aging*, 1992, Vol. 4, No. 1, p. 77.

Audio-Visual Resources

Johnson, Kerry, *The Science of Self-Discipline*. Nightingale-Conant Corp., PO Box 845, Morton Grove, IL 60053-9921 (PH 1 (800) 525-9000).

❖ Chapter Thirteen ❖
Familial and Marital Issues

Definition: *The sum total of the compatibility, companionship, support and satisfaction derived from your marriage (or special friendship) and your family.*

We are people of relationships. The degree to which we feel joy, delight, sensitivity, sharing and warmth from our families and special (marital) relationships is generally a good measure of our overall level of happiness. Our worlds are only partially fulfilling when we feel pain, anger, frustration, disappointment, hurt, guilt or fear in our families or special relationships. At such times we feel fragmented and experience an unsettling sense of confusion within. We seem to need connectedness in our lives to be as emotionally healthy and personally fulfilled as we can be.

Myron

Myron is 62. He has worked for 32 years for a large aerospace/defense contractor and has achieved no small level of success in a variety of positions there. Currently, he is chief of overseas personnel operations, a job which periodically takes him to rather exotic lands. Myron likes his job, but he also realizes that it has been, at best, a lateral promotion. In fact, none of his three "promotions" in the last 15 years could be considered advancements in the corporation. He knows that at one time he had been considered for VP of Human Resources, but was not selected. Since that time, his career seemed to reach a plateau. It's not that his work is boring or make-do. No, his positions have been valuable and contributing positions. It's just that they are not the "fast track," visible positions which lead to the big promotions. In a way, Myron knows he has been passed over and is simply using his experiences as best he can until he retires.

Actually, Myron is very interested in retirement. He has read books on retirement and maintains friendships with some of his retired colleagues from work. He even has plans for retirement. He wants to rekindle his love of planes and flying, a love that prompted him to start with an aerospace company in the first place. His retirement plans all seem in place. Even financially he will be able to make the move! Everything would be great in fact, if it were not for one big problem. Myron and his wife simply tolerate each other. Weekends around the house are more like marathons of avoidance. Myron and his wife eat their meals at the same table in stony silence. They rarely go out together, they share very little and their sexual intimacy is sparse indeed. Every time Myron starts thinking about his retirement, it doesn't feel at all like a time of personal expansion and development. When he is really honest with himself, in fact, it feels more like an impending prison sentence. Each time he tries to get concrete about his retirement plans, he crashes into the reality of his conflicted marital relationship, which shuts down the whole process like an aborted take-off. Myron is stuck, as well as fearful, frustrated and dismayed.

Medical researchers are now discovering what many have known all along: persons in satisfying relationships are simply healthier people! Generally, these people take increased pleasure in life, even if the pleasures are quiet ones. People in satisfying relationships actually contract fewer illnesses. When these folks do become sick, they recuperate sooner. For example, happily married men who experience a heart attack are able to bounce back more quickly and with less pronounced debilitation than unattached men or those with less than nurturant relationships. This, of course, is not always true for every individual. Many other variables color the health picture, but, in general, it's a fact that "lovers" are healthier people. Our very immune systems seem to protect us from outside invaders better when we feel the warmth and support of a caring relationship. On the other hand, the stress generated from a conflicted relationship can inhibit our immune system—leaving us more vulnerable to outside attack and illness. In short, a loving, compassionate relationship seems to be a health giving state for humans.

The ability to form and sustain a special, loving relationship is one of the premier characteristics of an emotionally healthy individual. The problems we encounter in our attempts to do just that fuel a never-ending list of songs, plays, movies, "soaps" and novels. Our search for affection has both made and ruined many a career. Indeed, our search has brought down governments and stopped promising political campaigns dead in their tracks. Our quest for tenderness, affiliation, affection, nurturance, connectedness and love is the central theme which runs through our history and our lives, alternately keeping us glued together or breaking us into pieces. Our fortunes seem to rise and fall on the tide of our relationships. Few things can bring us so much joy, as well as the potential for intense sorrow, as can our "love lives." Since this is true for the whole of life, it is no less true for retirement.

Relationship to Retirement

There's an old adage which sums up the impact of relationships on retirement, and visa versa: "I married him for better or for worse, but not for lunch!" Absence does make the heart grow fonder, and in many relationships "familiarity breeds contempt." Most married folks love their spouses, but somehow that spark of love can diminish when we're over-exposed to it. Like a photo that's been exposed to too much light, your relationship can become faded with too much togetherness. Even the best of relationships can suffer from overexposure.

Married couples have some particular problems in this area. In the traditional marriage, the man's domain is his work and perhaps the outside of the house, especially the basement and garage. The woman's domain is inside. Obviously, tremendous overlap exists in many relationships, but, nonetheless, this division of labor prevails to a greater or lesser degree. When the man retires, he loses a great chunk of his domain. If this were not stressful enough, he makes matters worse by invading his spouse's domain. The lifestyle shift which the man feels so dramatically is felt in a much less acute way by the woman, except for the fact that "he is underfoot." The necessary adjustment here can cause no small strain on any relationship.

George and Marie

George and Marie are happily married and have lived in a peaceful northeastern suburb for 25 years. Their one son is married with his own children and lives out-of-state. George worked for a large multi-national corporation. He was always punctual, conscientious, personable and a real "company man." He liked his job and they liked him. When retirement came upon George, perhaps a bit sooner than he had anticipated, he hadn't dreamed of the impact it would have on Marie!

Marie likes to read; George knows this. She is an intelligent person who enjoys all sorts of books. She is a regular at the local library and could easily spend between three to four hours daily sitting quietly reading. This seemed to be her therapy. She is not at all lazy, far from it. She is, on the contrary, quite efficient and probably gets more done on any given day, even with three or four hours taken out, than most people. Marie likes quiet. But even Marie hadn't realized how important to her was this "quiet time" until George's actual retirement came! Then she knew!

George likes things in order. He likes to putter, organize, arrange, set-up, structure things, etc. He is the living example of "a place for everything and everything in its place." You guessed it! Upon his retirement, George almost immediately launched into a campaign to reorder, restructure and rearrange the entire house. George also likes to have a helper, and Marie had always been the dutiful "consultant/gofer" for all of George's projects. In previous times, George's projects would be interrupted by his work, and Marie could order her own life to fit her reading time. Now that George doesn't go to work, his projects and his need of Marie to play the admiring helpmate seems unending. The stage was set for conflict.

George and Marie have spent several months feeling more than a small degree of strain. Each of them, in fact, has had fleeting thoughts of setting up their own residences. Only after the strain finally erupted into pitched battle, marked by weeping and distressed feelings formerly alien to this marriage, did George and Marie reach an understanding and a truce. George decided he had to do something to get out of the house. Marie, of course, agreed without hesitation. George went on to organize a retired men's community action group, which has since accomplished much in their small community. Marie is back to smiling at George as he leaves in the morning and arrives back in the afternoon, once again content to have "her time" to read.

Most persons retire as a couple. Even if you are not "coupled," there are always other persons in your life who are affected by your new lifestyle. Even if your spouse is still working when you retire, your new time schedule alone impacts on him or her very much. Your retirement decision and your preretirement planning is a joint affair. You must reach a consensus on so many issues related to the time of your retirement as well as your post-retirement lifestyle. If there is any communication barrier in your relationship, this will greatly stifle your clear and direct interchange, as well as inhibit the agreements so necessary for a smooth retirement decision and transition to occur. The future prospect of living in this tension-filled (or more likely avoidant) relationship is more than enough to sabotage your retirement plans and cause you to postpone or put off this life step. When there is disagreement or emotional withdrawal in your relationship, the prospect of the "good life" in retirement is simply absent.

The compatibility and companionship of your primary, special, intimate, relationship is a key factor in your ultimate retirement success. Retirement pushes you as a couple into dramatically proximate positions, so much more than you had experienced during your working years. Such constant closeness, without the benefit of a daily break of separation formerly provided by work, exerts a profound stress upon any relationship. This strain can cause havoc in "good" relationships! If yours has any known "flaws," this strain can be devastating.

Projection for Success in Retirement

Families and relationships can be evaluated along many different functions. However, three categories seem to stand out. The three are:

1. Cohesion
2. Adaptability
3. Communication

COHESION speaks to the sense of togetherness in a family and/or relationship. To what degree does the couple function together? Are they independent operators who basically do things separately, even if they are physically together? Or, do they operate as a team in their lives and in what they do? ADAPTABILITY has to do with the level of flexibility in the family or relationship. How well can the couple deal with change? Is it rigid, or more accepting? Finally, COMMUNICATION deals with sharing. How well does this family and/or couple share? This applies to all types of sharing: information, emotions, material things, their very persons and bodies (in sexual intimacy), their friends, their space, etc.?

Your RSP

Most people score quite high on their Expectations scale. Strong and close relationships, as we have pointed out, are a primary human need. Couples seem to have little disagreement with this goal, their only "rub" is with the means to achieve it. So, it's no surprise that you're probably like most people and have a high Expectations score.

Your PB (Present Behavior) Score may be different, because it is your evaluation of the quality of your relationship and family life right now. If you scored higher on the PB-scale, you undoubtedly rate the compatibility in your marital or special relationship as quite high. You probably have developed a good sense of team play, i.e., "we're in this thing together." Your cohesion is good. Likewise, your level of flexibility is probably good; your partner and you have worked out ways of adjusting to each other's wants and needs and look out for each other. You can negotiate well—each of you is probably able to give-and-take when necessary. Finally, your ways of sharing yourselves have been worked out to each other's satisfaction. You can exchange thoughts, feelings, fears and even secrets with relative security and comfort. You probably anticipate that retirement will bring changes to your relationship and your family, but you're probably confident that your bonds are strong enough, your relationship flexible enough, and your communication open enough to weather the storm.

Persons who score high on Factor Thirteen are generally in a healthy primary or marital relationship and can look to their partnership as a source of continuing strength and stability in their coming years of retirement. You have, in all probability, shared a quality relationship with your spouse (intimate other) for some time and look forward to sharing even more in retirement. Your projected success in retirement will be high.

If you scored lower on the PB-scale, you probably want to select this retirement success factor as one of focused concern. Your lower score says that there is potential for negative feelings, such as conflict, loneliness and/or resentment to surface in your relationship and/or family. Lower scores may eventually mean a level of emotional withdrawal in the future, if it hasn't occurred already. Lower scores indicate that this area requires careful examination now, before your retirement adds additional stress and strain. Finally, lower scores may indicate an insensitivity or a denial of the importance of your primary relationship in the entire scheme of success you want to achieve in retirement.

This factor is rather straightforward, i.e., it stands alone in measuring a very personal aspect of your life. However, we cannot overstate the very high predictive value this factor has for you and your retirement. Normally, when your PB-score is low here, you will find several other scores low, also. They are:

- Factor 1 – Disengagement from Work
- Factor 2 – Attitude Toward Retirement
- Factor 6 – Current Life Satisfaction
- Factor 7 – Projected Life Satisfaction

Strategies for Change

1. Assess the situation.

Find out to what degree your spouse (special relationship) feels as you do. Relationships are, of course, a mutual affair. You can't have a satisfying relationship with one partner pulling the weight of both. Ask your spouse some stimulating questions about your relationship. Better yet, each of you write a "state of the relationship" position paper. After you have read each other's papers, write down three changes you would like your spouse to make which would substantially enrich your relationship. Also write three changes you would be willing to make which you believe your partner would like you to make. Exchange these lists and develop a pact to actually commit to achieving these goals, not simply to please your partner, but to enhance your relationship.

2. Gather ideas and information.

Browse your local bookstore for titles that promise to help make relationships better. Some are better than others, but all have some value and can spark ideas and small changes in behavior which could have a marvelously positive impact on your relationship. We recommend that you and your partner read the book together, perhaps reading it aloud, alternating paragraphs, all the while applying selected ideas to your relationship.

3. Recognize each other's needs.

If there is one characteristic that all successful relationships share in common, it is respect. Respect means understanding the individual needs of your partner and helping him/her meet those needs. Respect means going the extra mile when it's required, but remaining silent all those other times when your impulse is to offer "constructive criticism" or "helpful feedback." Respect means recognizing the specialness and the individual humanness of your partner and allowing him/her to express uniqueness in this relationship. Respect means everything in a successful relationship.

4. See a professional if necessary.

If you recognize that your relationship has long-standing problems which you have tried to address on your own without success, seek the assistance of a professional counselor. Such a move is not an admission of failure or that you are some terrible person. Seeing someone who has the knowledge and competence to evaluate the specific concerns and problems you share, as well as the skills to help you and your partner bring about change, may invite healing and peace to a situation over which you have long struggled. Do it now, before the strain of retirement brings your concerns to a festering head. We believe that even the most successful and "together" relationships can benefit greatly from the help of a professional counselor who understands marriage and family dynamics—and the potential pressures of retirement as well.

Suggested Resources

Bianchi, Eugene C., Ruether, Rosemary R., *From Machismo to Mutuality*. New York: Paulist Press, 1976.

Buscaglia, Leo, *Living, Loving and Learning*. New York: Charles B. Slack, 1982.

Buscaglia, Leo, *Love*. New York: Fawcett Crest/Ballantine, 1982.

Cliff, Dallas R., "Under the Wife's Feet: Renegotiating Gender Divisions in Early Retirement," *Sociological Review*, Feb 1993, Vol. 41, No. 1, p. 30.

Clinebell, Howard J., *Growth Counseling for Mid-Years Couples*, Philadelphia: Fortress Press, 1971.

Johnson, Richard P., "Challenge to the Middle Years Marriage," Chapter in *Convergence, Generations in the Middle*, Warren Scott (Ed.), pp. 114–126, Kansas City, MO: Mid-America Congress on Aging, 1988.

Miller, Lawrence E., "Invasion of the Retired Spouse," *New Choices for Retirement Living*, Feb 1992, Vol. 32, No. 1, p. 74.

Peck, M. Scott, *The Road Less Traveled*. New York: Simon & Schuster, 1978.

Audio-Visual Resources

Buscaglia, Leo, *Loving Each Other*. Nightingale-Conant Corp., PO Box 845, Morton Grove, IL 60053-9921 (PH 1 (800) 525-9000).

❖ Chapter Fourteen ❖ Perception of Age

Definition: *Your view of your ability (or lack) to perform and achieve in relation to your age, i.e., how young or old do you feel?*

Bob

Bob is 39 years old. He is part of an advertising agency considered by many to be one of the best in the city. Bob has been in the firm four and a half years. He is well paid, professionally talented in the business, and considered by those outside his agency as a solid, attractive person who can be depended on. Emotionally, Bob is dying rapidly. He can barely get his energy up to go into the office, and, when he does get there, he now finds himself withdrawing and acting aloof. He cannot remember the last time he has come up with what he considered a really creative idea!

The reason for all this is clear to him. It began following the conversation he had with his boss eight or nine months ago. His boss had made it crystal clear to him that he was not going anywhere in this agency! He had been hired because he'd had an "in" with a very large account whose business was about to be taken over by this firm. They wanted Bob on board to handle that account. Period!

That was not what he had been told when he was first being courted to change positions and join this firm. Then, he was given visions of some day being vice presidential material and, in the future, even the possibility of a full partnership! They wanted HIM! They told Bob they wanted him because of his talent, training, experience and ability to work in a collegial style of office setting. Bob had fallen for it. He made the change, moved his family 500 miles, left his friends and support system, a good position that really would have led somewhere, and burned his bridges. This move was the big one for him. Now, he's 39. It was well known in the profession that if you are not in the big place by the time you are 40, you are not going to make it. Bob has to face facts and somehow get his life unstuck and moving again. Right now, he might be 39, but he feels 99!

Karen

Karen has never been this happy in her whole life! At age 67, she has lived through many changes in life. Now she is getting married! Imagine! At her age! When Bill died 24 years ago, she had never dreamed she would get married again. That marriage had been a good one. She and Bill had raised three children, done some traveling, and had enjoyed a nice life. Bill was killed in an industrial accident. At first it had been very hard for Karen; there were lots of adjustments to be made. But she made them. Financially, she had been able to live quite comfortably since Bill's death, as a result of the insurance money. In fact, she had lived very nicely. She had traveled, worked part-time for a while and then full-time when she found the right job. She had been able to visit the kids when she wanted to and had all the personal freedom one could ask for.

Larry was introduced to Karen by a friend. Somehow, they immediately knew this relationship was special. They laugh, they have similar likes, they are both solid in their single lives and do not "need" to get married. They just want to! Karen cannot believe it! Larry feels the same way. Getting married is just the thing they want to do. When Karen talks to her friends about it, her opening line is always, "You know, it's like I'm 17 years old again!" Karen might chronologically be 67, but emotionally she feels 17!

Bob and Karen are examples of the different levels upon which we live our lives. When we are having fun and are filled with excitement, we feel young and alive. When we are depressed and trapped by the circumstances of life, we feel old, sometimes very old. In our minds, with the intellectual understanding we possess, we know what our age is. However, our feelings take us up and down on a roller coaster of emotion. Sometimes the dips and depressions last a long time. Occasionally they become a way of life and we adopt a certain stance or approach toward life that others call "young." We get a certain reputation for "thinking young," or for "being young at heart"! The reverse, of course is also true. Sometimes we also can get a reputation for being "old"! Everyone knows examples of people who chronologically are in their 30's, but act and feel as if they are in their 70's! This Perception of Age factor has much to do with your retirement decision.

Relationship to Retirement

We all have a sense of how old we feel. In casual conversations between friends you'll often hear one ask the other, "Jim, how old do you feel you are?" And Jim will be able to quickly respond with a specific figure! We all distinguish between our chronological age and our emotional or feeling age. The psychological category of one's "functional age," i.e., your perceived ability to perform, is a good one to help define this concept further. A person's functional age is normally used to describe the developing capabilities of children; it refers to their level of maturation and achievement to date. Factor 14 seeks to measure what you think you can do, based on your view of your own age. Are you old for your years or young for them?

This factor uncovers your perception of what is young or old. Age here is used as a measure of the "wear and tear" you have so far experienced from life. To what degree do you feel you are worn? This is the basic question of Factor 14.

Factor 14 relates to retirement in very direct ways. Persons who feel older than their chronological years are more inclined to retire earlier. This, of course, assumes all other retirement success factors remain constant. Continuing to work requires some level of energy and vitality. If you feel you do not have that kind of energy, you will be much more inclined to leave the job and the demands of that routine.

Your attitude toward your own aging also has a direct bearing on your retirement decision. The degree to which you associate aging with decreased performance can effect your retirement timing. For instance, if you believe that retirement is the first step toward senility, or that you will "age" in retirement, you will probably want to put off retirement as long as possible in an attempt to avoid your own aging. (Do you remember the story of Bill and Margery in Chapter 2? Margery's attitude toward retirement was greatly affected by her father's rapid health deterioration in retirement.) If, on the other hand, you feel you do need a rest and the only way you can see yourself getting it is by retiring, you will probably go directly to the door with few stops along the say. You are tired! You really want to get home! This job is in your way!

Let's take a look now at what the scores mean and how they could impact your level of retirement readiness. Your Expectations score, or the score you believe you will achieve in your life at retirement, is easy to understand. The higher your score, the more positively you feel about your current chronological age in life. It is an indication of your high energy level and a vitality that embraces life. It also makes a very positive statement about your sense of how well you perform and function in comparison with your peer group.

Lower scores on the Expectations score indicate the level, or degree, to which you feel tired and "shop worn." Lower scores point toward a pessimistic and discouraged attitude toward age and suggest a belief system that undermines confidence in your ability to perform and compete successfully with others in life and your work environment.

Lower scores on the second scale, or the Present Behaviors scale, indicate a sense of feeling older than would be appropriate for a person with your chronological age. Feeling older, you also have a conviction that you no longer perform or do your job competitively. This posture, or belief system, pushes you toward retirement so you can rest. Rest is an important consideration because you often feel tired! Also, because you cannot see your situation changing, you are pushed to leave the demands and obligations of your work environment. Retiring, or leaving the job behind, may seem like the only way to escape and get the rest you feel you need!

If your scores are higher on the Present Behaviors scale, you indicate a willingness to keep on going! You feel good about your actual chronological age and feel competent and able to meet the challenges and demands of work and life around you. Your energy level is high and you retain an enthusiasm for life and work. You may, in fact, feel that you are performing at a higher level than ever before in your work history!

Projection for Success in Retirement

Person who score lower on the PB scale of Factor 14 are motivated to retire sooner rather than later. These same persons normally score lower on the E-scale. This combination describes a person who "feels old" and believes their abilities to perform on the job are severely compromised. Because they basically feel "tired" and "shop-worn," their energy level is lower, resulting in reduced activity. Those whose scores fall into this pattern will be drawn toward an earlier retirement and, once in retirement, will favor a more quiet, sedentary style of retirement living. They will not be spontaneous or eager to explore new activities, preferring a lifestyle that accents rest and quietness.

In contrast, persons who score higher on the PB scale of this factor are persons who feel able and interested in keeping things going! They feel good about their current age and could never be accused of feeling older than their chronological years. These people usually score very high on the E-scale, indicating a strong sense of energy and vitality. They believe they currently perform and achieve at a very significant level. If they choose to retire, their chances of becoming a "retread" (getting another job) are quite high.

People who have higher E scores and PB scores are most likely to enjoy an active retirement where the emphasis will be on movement and productivity. People who have lower E scores and PB scores, in contrast, will favor an earlier retirement date and choose a more sedentary lifestyle, emphasizing rest rather than activity. Factor 14 is the only factor which must be understood in consideration with all the other factors. It is directly influenced by all the other factors.

Our work at the Center for Retirement Success convinces us that persons who feel young and have high energy levels (higher E scores and PB scores) will have the greatest opportunities to achieve overall retirement success. Having energy, enthusiasm and the desire to do things in an active, inquiring way, contributes heavily to the enjoyment of life. If you are interested in moving your life more in this direction, consider these suggestions:

Strategies for Change

1. Make an assessment of the current level of activity in your lifestyle.

Actually sit down with paper and pencil and write down the activities you are involved in. Especially consider physical activities. Are you active on a regular basis? Are you doing things necessary to keep weight down and energy up? Have you mastered the art of eating less? Do you do the right things to give your body a chance to feel good and build up its energy level? Give this whole area careful thought.

2. Find ways to increase your level of activity.

Make a list of possible activities you could see yourself participating in. Select several of them and actually do them. Stepping up your pace will promote energy and an over-all feeling of well-being. Find a physician who exercises and will help you to increase your general level of wellness in this important area of your life. Many physicians will encourage and assist you if you take the initiative. If yours will not, get a second opinion.

3. Do what younger people are doing on occasion.

Actually mixing with younger people stimulates and promotes healthy growth. You do not have to do it all the time; just often enough to remind yourself how refreshing it is when you begin and how good it feels when you quit!

4. Be certain you use current information about aging to inform the decisions you make.

Again, remember how important our beliefs about aging become to our activity schedules. Remember:

a. Only 5% of Americans over age 65 are in nursing homes at any one time.

b. Only 5% of Americans over age 65 have Alzheimer's disease or any other kind of senility.
c. Life expectancy today is nearly age 80 for women and over age 72 for men . . . . up from about age 45 for both sexes at the turn of the century.
d. Today we are making plans for a whole new additional half of life! And it's an opportunity not for only a few exceptional people, but for everyone.

Factor 14 contributes greatly to your life enjoyment. Do what is necessary to get this factor balanced and working for you in a healthful way!

Suggested Resources

Arn, Win, and Arn, Charles, *Live Long and Love It!* Wheaton, IL: Tyndale House Publ., 1991.

Cooper, Kenneth, *The Aerobic Program for Total Well Being*. New York: McEvans & Co., Inc., 1982.

Cooper, Kenneth, *The Aerobics Way*. New York: Bantam Books, 1978.

Ekerdt, David J., and Deviney, Stanley, "Evidence for a Preretirement Process Among Older Male Workers," *Journals of Gerontology*, Mar 1993, Vol. 48, No. 2, p. S35.

Kopp, Sheldon, *Mirror, Mask and Shadow; The Risks and Rewards of Self-Acceptance*. New York: Bantam Books, 1982.

Laslett, Peter, *Fresh Map of Life: The Emergence of the Third Age*. Cambridge, MA: Harvard Univ. Press, 1991.

Morley, Robert, *Pleasures of Age*. San Francisco, CA: Mercury House, 1990.

Rubin, T., *Reconciliations; Inner Peace in an Age of Anxiety*. Berkley Books, 1982.

Scott, D., *How To Put More Time in Your Life*. New York: Signet, 1981.

Selye, Hans, *The Stress of Life*, 2nd Ed. New York: McGraw-Hill, 1978.

Audio-Visual Resources

Oechsli, Matt, *Reevaluating Your Life*. Nightingale-Conant Corp., PO Box 845, Morton Grove, IL 60053-9921 (PH 1 (800) 525-9000).

❖ Chapter Fifteen ❖
Replacement of Work Functions

Definition: *The degree to which you have planned to replace the five functions of work.*

Working serves many different functions for each of us who works. In general, however, there exist five recognized functions of work. They are:

1. Financial stability
2. Time management
3. Sense of utility
4. Socialization
5. Status

Each of us derives benefits from these factors to varying degrees. The value we place on each determines the priority of the five functions for us. Let's look at these separately.

1. Financial stability.

For most of us, work is the major source of our income. Our labor provides us with a steady flow of monetary support. Permanent employment, with its fringe benefits of health insurance, pension plan, vacation and holiday pay and the like buffer us from financial catastrophe by absorbing us into a continuing channel of compensation. Our employment allows us to tap that channel for support, much like a city taps a river for its source of water.

2. Time management.

Work also structures our lives. It normally makes continuous and regular demands of our time. Because of our work, most of us needn't devote much energy to deciding what to do, or where to go when Monday morning rolls around again. The time management function that work provides (and which so many of us complain about) keeps our lives orderly and somehow "in-sync" with the beat of our economy and society. Managing our time keeps us in the mainstream of life around us.

3. Sense of utility.

Third, work gives us purpose. Whatever the content of our work, we derive a primary sense of accomplishment from it. In a sense, work gives us a "cause" to follow. Most of us want to think well of ourselves, and it is from our work, with its productivity, that we receive a quantitative measure of worth. We achieve this sense of worth not simply from the monetary benefits, but also from the personal benefits of knowing that we do something of value. In addition, if our work did not provide something of value to our society, there would be no wages attached to it.

4. Socialization.

Most of our work brings us into close, if not constant, contact with other people. This association fills our most basic human need: socialization—connecting with other people. Indeed, some anthropologists believe that the work relationships we form are precisely the means humans use to bring about higher and higher levels of civilization. Humans seem to be able to conceive of ever greater projects which require ever increasing cooperation among people. We have even entered the time of multi-national and even multi-cultural corporations, heading, it seems, toward a world economy. All of this requires understanding, association, affiliation, negotiation and constant human communications.

5. Status.

Finally, our work gives us status in the community. Our peers know who we are to a large measure by what we do. We seem to define ourselves first by our occupation or profession. Likewise, we are regarded or measured in the community by the value of the service we provide to it. This value is not simply measured in dollars, it is afforded as a form of status. Most of our religious leaders, ministers, priests, rabbis, sisters, etc., are highly valued, i.e., they enjoy considerable status. Yet, they are not normally financially rewarded to any great degree. Status is that measure of worth and identity we receive from our peers. It is an internal quality as a consequence of our work, aside and apart from its monetary value. This can be more important to us than we first imagine. It's very important that we know who we are in relation to others; our work gives us that measure of comparison.

Carol

Until Carol's husband had a stroke at the early age of 45, she had helped him keep the books of his small cement contracting business. After the shock of his medical disability became bearable to her, and she realized that she couldn't keep the business, she enrolled in medical assistant school. One year later, she is working in a large medical office preparing people to see the many doctors who practice there.

She likes her job. Certainly she, her husband Bob and their two children need the money she makes, not to mention the health care benefits she and her family receive. Carol doesn't necessarily relish getting up each morning to fight the traffic she confronts daily, but there is a certain regularity to her life that she hadn't experienced when she was at home. Further, she feels like she is doing something very meaningful. Her role in the medical care delivery system is a front-line role. It gives her the opportunity to continuously learn more about new advances in health care. She likes keeping her skill level sharp and strong.

Carol also meets many nice people. Not only does she like her work mates, but she now has relationships with the doctors and nurses, something her old career could never have offered. She relates well to all the patients who visit the office; she feels like a friend to a few of them. Finally, she seems to have more of a clear sense of who she is as an individual. Sometimes, in the morning traffic, she suddenly experiences a warming sense that she is in the mainstream of life, just like all these other people on the highway. She is somebody! She glances at herself in the exam room mirrors, taking note of her white uniform, and feels a sense of pride for being the best medical assistant she can be!

Relationship to Retirement

It's important that you fully recognize all the benefits and rewards that your work provides you, because in retirement, you will lose them. The plans you develop to address this loss is the central theme of this last retirement success factor.

In order for you to retire with a sense of security about the future, it's necessary to have some plans, however rudimentary, so you can replace the functions formerly satisfied by work. The degree to which you have accomplished this is the degree to which you will feel increasingly comfortable approaching retirement. Without plans to address these potential losses, you are courting a possible emptiness in retirement.

Some people look toward retirement with a great sense of relief that they will be unshackled from the constraints imposed upon them by their work. Certainly, a degree of this anticipation is normal and healthy in that it will excite you about your new life in retirement. However, it is possible for this sense to be carried to an extreme degree where you lose sight of the benefits you derive from work. When and if this occurs, you may race toward retirement as the panacea (cure all) for all your ills. When you approach retirement with such an attitude, you tend to undermine your planning process to the degree that you discount the necessity for completeness. In short, when you run headlong toward a goal simply seeking relief from an oppressive situation, you neglect to clearly project the consequences of your action after you reach your goal. You may succeed in getting out of working, but also find yourself in an empty shell of a life.

Some people seem to forget that this retirement stage of their life has emerged from the foundation of life experience they have built all through those previous years! Whatever ways you choose to develop and manage this segment of your life differently from former stages in your life, it is nonetheless a continuation of your life. You are still the same person with the same personality in retirement that you were before. You may have a new lifestyle, but it's still you! You still have your same particular way of looking at the world that remains constant and continuous. This continuity is important and needs to be remembered, because you will have the same wants, needs and desires after your retirement as you did before. That's why this last retirement success factor is so vital to your continued success as an individual person. You will continue to need to fulfill the five rewards you formerly achieved through working in other new ways which you will determine in retirement.

Juan

Juan is a 55 year-old life-long insurance representative. He works for a major corporation and has always made a steady, better than average living. He alternately praises his work and damns it. He has, in the past, explored other lines of work, never actually giving up his position, but certainly investigating others rather thoroughly. He invariably returns to his decision that he is where he needs to stay.

Juan's work does provide him with financial stability. Furthermore, Juan has unfortunately developed a chronic, non-debilitating illness, which requires continuous medical management. His company-paid health benefits have become vastly more valuable to him since he contracted this illness. Juan's time is his own, he controls his schedule. He often says that he could never work a 9–5 job. Juan needs this time flexibility and his position affords that to him. His work also provides him with an easy measure of his utility and productivity. His weekly sales figures are an accurate, direct (and sometimes stinging) measurement of his level of production.

Juan also likes meeting and dealing with the clients whom he serves. His sales calls are more likely to be face-to-face visits. Talking about life insurance and investment needs brings Juan in very close touch with the pulse of life. He shares his views, ideas and sometimes even his short-comings with his clients, and they with him. He recognizes the value of this interaction in his life and he clearly appreciates the richness that this aspect of his job adds to life.

Finally, Juan has status. He is somebody! He is aware that he carries the banner of his company, and all that it stands for, around with him. Juan rather enjoys wearing his company lapel pin on his suit jacket, and is keenly aware of its presence, especially when he is around groups of people at church, the civic and fraternal organization meetings, at ball games and even social functions with his wife. He gets a glow of action, and really feels like somebody in the community when he personally delivers the insurance benefit check to the surviving spouse. More often, he delivers the checks to widows who have recently lost their husbands. Juan knows how much this money is needed, and regards it as a gift from the deceased spouse to his/her surviving partner. In a way, Juan feels like an emissary from above, on a mission of mercy to rescue those in need. At times like these, there is no question that Juan feels an undeniable status as a vital part of his community.

Your RSP

Assessing your level of preparation on this factor is somewhat difficult on two levels. The first is that you may not have ever thought about the rewards of work you receive in quite this way before. Second, you are lumping five different values (the five rewards of work) into one overall satisfaction measure.

Persons who score higher on Factor Fifteen are better prepared to enter retirement because they have projected their personal and financial needs more clearly than those who score lower on the factor. High scorers recognize the shift that must take place in the way they have met their needs before retirement and how they will meet them after retirement. Low scorers either have given little thought to this impending shift or they simply have so far failed to act on their thinking. In either case, they are less likely to achieve the same level of success in retirement as high scorers are likely to achieve.

Ironically, persons who have lower scores on Factor Fifteen may retire earlier than high scorers, not because they are more ready, but rather the contrary. Low scorers have not planned as comprehensively and run the risk of developing a false or narrow sense of security about this new life phase they are about to enter. Consequently, they may be "the fools who rush in where angels fear to tread." High scorers will be more cautious regarding their retirement timing, preferring to wait until their plans are more solidified and pragmatic.

Other retirement success factors which might illuminate your analysis of Factor 15 are:

- Factor 1 – Work Disengagement
- Factor 2 – Attitude Toward Retirement
- Factor 5 – Financial Security
- Factor 6 – Current Life Satisfaction
- Factor 9 – Leisure Interests

Jack

Jack retired four years ago from a large chemical corporation. He had been with them over 28 years and had helped to shepherd the company from a regional industrial chemical producer into a multi-national concern with interests at every level of the R & D, production, distribution and marketing facets of the industry. Indeed, Jack was on the front lines of this growth. He was shifted from new plant to new plant as the set-up supervisor. His job was to insure that the plant opened and became functional in all aspects in the shortest possible time. This position brought him in close contact with all echelons of the corporation management, from human resources, new construction, maintenance, operations and community relations, to the highest managerial levels.

Jack's position was a high-powered, high-stress job upon which he had always thrived. His five functions of work were more than fulfilled; most of the time they were overflowing. In fact, the only time Jack didn't care for his job was when he was "stuck" at the corporate headquarters preparing to move out to a new plant site and begin the building process all over again. Needless to say, Jack was highly regarded and exceptionally well rewarded for his contributions to the corporation.

Inevitably, the build-up process slowed down. Jack reached the 60 year mark, and an administrative downsizing decision precipitated the offer of an early retirement opportunity. Jack's accountant urged him to accept the package because the accountant thought it a "good deal."

What appeared a "good package" for Jack turned out to be a "raw deal." Four months after Jack retired, he found himself in his family physician's office with complaints of tiredness, insomnia, decreased appetite, increased irritability, weight loss and loss of interest in life. His doctor informed Jack that he was clinically depressed. The anti-depressant medication and short-term counseling recommended were not enough to snap Jack out of his malaise. Eventually, Jack was admitted onto the psychiatric floor of the local hospital for treatment of a major depressive disorder. It was during his 4 1/2 week stay there that Jack truly grappled with what had been gnawing at him for some time. His work had been his life! Now that it was over, Jack somehow felt hollow, empty, useless and without purpose. Through good treatment from the medical team and support from his wife, Jack gradually built a new retirement lifestyle. He incorporated alternate ways to address and replace the factors from his work life, in which he had invested so heavily, and which he had so sorely missed. He began a new life.

Strategies for Change

1. Review your financial plan with a financial planner.

Reassess and reevaluate your retirement expense needs. Is your plan able to sustain the level of income necessary for your projected lifestyle? Project the realistic income you can expect from: a. Social Security, b. your company pension plan and c. your personal savings and investments. Some expenses like carfare and clothing generally decrease after retirement. Others, such as health costs, entertainment, travel and household expenses may, in fact, increase.

2. Develop a time schedule.

You may not feel this is necessary; indeed, you may feel the reason you are retiring is to get away from schedules. Such an attitude will discourage your success in retirement. While a certain slackening in your time schedule would be advisable, completely unstructured time breeds lack-lustre satisfaction, lethargy and a lost sense of purpose in life. Your need for thoughtful time management is no less critical in retirement than it was when you were actively on-the-job—if not more so!

3. Develop and stick to your goals.

Develop both long-term and short-term goals in each of the six life arenas. (You may want to review chapters six and seven.) Organize specific objectives that are observable, time-limited, measurable and realistic for each goal which will serve as a blue-print, as steps toward your goal accomplishment. While you are working, many of your behavioral objectives and performance goals are well (and sometimes not so well) outlined for you in your job description. What is your retirement job description? If you don't have one . . . construct one; if you can't construct one, you probably won't get to where you want to go because you won't know where that is. The fact is, you need to extend that sense of utility you have on-the-job into your retirement . . . without it, you're lost!

4. Maintain past friendships and develop new ones.

One of the many myths about retirement is that you will continue to socialize with the same group from the office, plant, shop, store, etc., that you have socialized with all along. Many unfortunate retirees discover that they never realized how much of the conversation that occurs at work is "shop-talk." After retirement, your source of new "shop-talk" is cut off. You may find to your disappointment that your level of participation in the banter with work-buddies diminishes after you retire. You still play a vital role during these times, and your former co-workers still want to see you and enjoy having you around. Remember, however, that your information is just not as fresh as theirs; you may feel a certain sense of detachment. It's important to recognize this as being normal and not let it bar you from participation. This is why it's so important to develop new social groups. A successful retirement lifestyle demands decisions, determination and doing!

5. Find a "cause" and doggedly pursue it.

One mistake often made by novice retirees is to think they are going to rest. Certainly retirement affords you time to rest and relax; without a question, this is important. Equally, and perhaps more important, is to discover, to rediscover and/or to continue to pursue your cause on an increased level. A great man once said, "When I rest (too much), I rust!"

Each of us needs a cause, a means to funnel our energies to make our world a better place. We have an innate drive to help people. In our "me-generation" world, we're tempted to believe that altruism, helping others for the innate pleasure of helping, is dead. Recent research is clear, those people who give of their time and talents, without worrying about payment, are the most healthy folks among us. Even after the researchers control for such factors as age, lifelong health, religious preference, family background, etc., the data are clear. Those who help others . . . are healthier! Does this mean that the more you help, the healthier you will be? We don't know that yet, but we do know that helping others helps you. To give is to receive! We know that each of us needs to feel we're doing something in the community that is vital!

In retirement we need a role. We had a role when we were working and that need is no less evident today. What will your retirement role be? You're the author, director, camera person and actor of your retirement. In the final analysis, you're also the judge and jury!

Suggested Resources

Bikson, Tora K., Goodchilds, J. D., Huddy, L., Eveland, J. D., and Schneider, S., *Networked Information Technology and the Transition to Retirement: A Field Experiment*. Santa Monica, CA: Rand, 1991.

Crabtree, Darryl A., Antrim, Laura R., and Klenke, Rita, "Effects of Activity Levels on Controlled Information Processing in Older Adults," *Activities, Adaptation and Aging*, 1990, Vol. 14, No. 3, p. 77.

Danigelis, N. L. and McIntosh, B. R., "Resources and the Productive Activity of Elders—Race and Gender As Contexts," *Journals of Gerontology*, Jul 1993, Vol. 48, No. 4, p. 192.

Ellis, John R., "Volunteerism as an Enhancement to Career Development," *Journal of Employment Counseling*, Sept 1993, Vol. 30, No. 3, p. 127.

Ethel, Edward, *The Best Time of Your Life*. E.O. Ethel, 1987.

Givechian, Fatemeh, *Work in Retirement: The Persistence of an American Collective Representation*. Lanham, MD: University Press of America, 1990.

Gould, R., *Transformations*. New York: Simon and Schuster, 1978.

Hepworth, M. and Featherstone, M., *Surviving Middle Age*. Basil Blackwell, 1982.

Kean, Rita C., VanZandt, Sally, and Maupin, Wendy, "Successful Aging: The Older Entrepreneur," *Journal of Women and Aging*, 1993, Vol. 5, No. 1, p. 25.

Scarf, M., *Unfinished Business: Pressure Points in the Lives of Women*. Ballantine, 1980.

Schultz, Carol M. and Galbraith, Michael W., "Community Leadership Education For Older Adults: An Exploratory Study," *Educational Gerontology*, Sept 1993, Vol. 19, No. 6, p. 473.

Sheehy, Gail, *Pathfinders*. New York: Bantam Books, 1982.

Audio-Visual Resources

Tracy, Brian, *How To Master Your Time*. Nightingale-Conant Corp., PO Box 845, Morton Grove, IL 60053-9921 (PH 1 (800) 525-9000).

❖ Conclusion ❖

This book is designed neither as an invitation to retire, nor as a request to continue working. Our goal has been, simply, to provide you with information to help you make the most informed and planned decision possible about your retirement. Our hope is that your decision will culminate in a successful and rewarding life experience for you and your family. We hope that the information and ideas we have given you here, have neither encouraged nor discouraged you from retirement, but rather have strengthened your confidence and conviction about your own future success.

As you have probably surmised from evaluating the information contained in this book, there is no one way to retire. Your retirement is as personal and unique as is your fingerprint. This flexibility to do whatever you want to do with this stage of your life is what makes retirement so completely different from any other life transition you have experienced. All the other stages have had, to a greater or lesser degree, an element of "you must," "you have to," "this is mandatory," or at least "you should," attached to them. Such directives are not part of the retirement scene. Some people take to this new-found freedom like a duck to water. Others almost drown in it! The fifteen retirement success factors, and particularly your own assessment of how you stack up to them, provides the most thorough and comprehensive evaluation you could have.

Planning For The Future

Now that you have taken the Retirement Success Profile, you have created for yourself a powerful new perspective on the career development stage of retirement. Look over your entire RSP. Where are your retirement strengths (those factors where you scored higher on the PB scale)? Where are your retirement concerns (those areas where you scored lowest on the PB scale)? Next, write down your top five retirement strengths as recorded on your profile.

Retirement Strengths (PB-Scales – Five Highest Scores):

1. ____________________

2. ____________________

3. ____________________

4. ____________________

5. ____________________

Next, write down five retirement concerns.

Retirement Concerns (PB-Scales – Five Lowest Scores):

1. ______________________________

2. ______________________________

3. ______________________________

4. ______________________________

5. ______________________________

Congratulate yourself for your strengths! You've worked hard and very conscientiously through life to achieve those scores. Your scores indicate you have done well in ways you may not have been aware of! You have strengths and you should feel good about them! In these strength areas, your only task now is to maintain those skills, keeping them ready to use as you need them in your retirement.

Now, what will you do about your retirement concerns (the lowest scores on your PB-scales)? For starters, look back to the corresponding chapters in this book which describe and outline your five retirement concerns. Choose one of the strategies for change listed in each chapter which seems most appropriate to help you raise your overall retirement readiness in each of these areas. Record it in the space below.

Retirement Concerns

1. Factor # ________

   Strategy for Change: ____________________________

   ____

   ____

   ____

   ____

2. Factor # ________

   Strategy for Change: ____________________________

   ____

   ____

   ____

   ____

3. Factor # ________

   Strategy for Change: ______________________

   ____

   ____

   ____

   ____

4. Factor # ________

   Strategy for Change: ______________________

   ____

   ____

   ____

   ____

5. Factor # ________

   Strategy for Change: ______________________

   ____

   ____

   ____

   ____

You have now created a preliminary retirement readiness "plan of action." At the very least, this plan can get you started toward achieving the highest level of success possible. Certainly, you'll want to modify your plans in response to changes you encounter along the way. However, you now have a grounded plan which has evolved from your own assessment. Having a plan like this is so important for you! We have been privileged, from our perspective through the years, to watch many, many people like you use this knowledge and these plans to raise their level of confidence about moving into that next phase of life. We are confident that it will happen for you, too!

But, what do you do if you know you're scheduled to retire very soon and won't have time to execute your plan? That is a very good question! It is one that is faced by many people, especially those who have recently accepted an early retirement window, which often affords them only a few weeks to make a decision. If you find yourself in this situation, you have two avenues of action open to you:

1. The first is to begin a new job search. You are certainly not forced to retire. Finding another position, if only a part-time one, is something that almost 50% of retirees opt for, at least in the early part of their retirement.
2. Second, you could prepare for your retirement lifestyle after you actually retire. Many, many retirees are not fully prepared to take the final step into retirement when their actual retirement date arrives. They are forced to formulate their retirement lifestyle "in-place," so to speak. You are fortunate because you already have a plan, based upon your work

> and learning in this book. This plan gives you a tremendous advantage in projecting your retirement success, regardless of whether you are still working or you have actually passed your retirement date. You could make the first few months of retirement your future lifestyle planning time. What you obviously want to avoid, and what has de-railed more than a few retirees, is entering your retirement with no plans at all, not even the plan to make a plan! It's in such situations that panic can set in and throw even the most stable retirees into turmoil.

In observing both retired and pre-retired persons, we have recognized something quite amazing. When people are given information of an accurate and personal nature, they seem to incorporate the fundamentals into themselves, effortlessly, and without even knowing it's happening! This is the validation of true "change information"! When truly relevant, honest and accurate information is made available, the entire being of the person seems to take it in. He or she automatically, instinctively begins the process of changing in the necessary direction. We humans genuinely want life to be good, and we make use of accurate information to help us find that good life! We know that you will do this too!